The complete paintings of

# Giorgione

Introduction by **Cecil Gould**

Notes and catalogue by **Pietro Zampetti**

Harry N. Abrams, Inc. *Publishers* New York

**Classics of the
World's Great Art**

**Editor**
Paolo Lecaldano

**International Advisory Board**
Gian Alberto dell'Acqua
André Chastel
Douglas Cooper
Lorenz Eitner
Enrique Lafuente Ferrari
Bruno Molajoli
Carlo L. Ragghianti
Xavier de Salas
David Talbot Rice
Jacques Thuillier
Rudolf Wittkower

*This series of books is
published in Italy by Rizzoli
Editore, in France by
Flammarion, in the United
Kingdom by Weidenfeld and
Nicolson, in the United States
by Harry N. Abrams, Inc., in Spain by
Editorial Noguer and in
Switzerland by Kunstkreis*

Standard Book Number 8109–5507–5
Library of Congress Catalogue
Card Number 74–92262
© Copyright in Italy by
Rizzoli Editore, 1968
Printed and bound in Italy

# Table of contents

*Photographic sources*     Colour plates: Ashmolean Museum, Oxford; Blauel, Munich; Emmer, Venice; Fine Arts Society, San Diego, California; Flammarion, Paris; Herzog Anton-Ulrich Museum, Brunswick; Meyer, Vienna; Museum Boymans-Van Beuningen, Rotterdam; National Gallery of Art, Washington, D.C.; Scala, Florence; Staatliche Museen, Berlin; Witty, Sunbury-on-Thames.
Black and white illustrations: Rizzoli archives, Milan; Emmer, Venice; Ferruzzi, Venice; Fiorentini, Venice; National Gallery of Ireland, Dublin; Rossi, Venice; Soprintendenza alle Gallerie, Naples.

# Introduction

The solid, undeniable facts concerning Giorgione could be contained without congestion on a postcard, and his surviving output is confined to a mere handful of pictures, most of them fairly small. Why, then, all the fuss? What accounts for the fame and the legend? Some of it, undoubtedly, springs from the very rarity of his pictures, and a great deal from the highly romantic image – the early death, and the fact that it was due to the plague said to have been caught from a lady friend. Something, again, is due to the romantic quality inherent in the paintings themselves – the fact that in some cases they depict mysterious and enigmatic subjects which have hitherto defied elucidation. But all this fails to add up to a total explanation, and the residue must surely be made up from the quality of the pictures themselves. Giorgione happened to live and work at a magic moment in Italian and Venetian art, when new ideas about Nature and God and Antiquity, and man's relation to them, were being discussed just when several generations of technical advance had given painters the full power of illustrating them. The result, among others, was the *Tempest*, the quintessential Giorgione.

The high quality of Giorgione's work, combined with the fact of his early death – irrespective of the exact circumstances in which it may have occurred – should have sufficed to start the legend. It did, indeed, emerge very soon. The demand for his work, for one thing, was always great. Immediately after Giorgione's death Isabella d'Este tried to get one of his pictures – no matter which – and even she was unable to do so. And as early as 1528 Giorgione is referred to by Castiglione in the same breath as Leonardo, Raphael and Michelangelo. There is also some evidence that within a few more years Giorgione's work was already being forged – a sure sign of esteem. In the next century – the seventeenth – the clothes of the lovers or music-makers in pictures by Giorgione, or attributed to him, started a fashion in costume – "alla Giorgion-esca" – which is met with in some of the early works of Caravaggio, and by this time, too, Giorgione had risen sufficiently high in the connoisseurs' canon to be endowed with a fictitious noble ancestry. Also in the seventeenth century the legend of Giorgione became linked with that of another and very different short-lived genius. This was Gaston de Foix, the brilliant French general who was killed in his hour of victory at the Battle of Ravenna in 1512, aged twenty-three. It is in the highest degree unlikely that Giorgione could ever have met him, and in any case Gaston's fame sprang principally from the circumstances of his death – which occurred two years after Giorgione's. Nevertheless pictures called "Gaston de Foix by Giorgione" proliferated in the seventeenth century and changed hands at high prices. Such is the persuasive power of the romantic imagination.

This and other picturesque embroideries succeeded to such an extent in obscuring both the real personality of Giorgione (of which, in fact, very little can be deduced) and the real authorship of most of the pictures optimistically attributed to him that when, in the late nineteenth century, methodical connoisseurship at last set to work to sift the true from the false it found itself faced with one of the most difficult problems in the history of art. Until about forty years ago the most reliable guide was the diary of Marcantonio Michiel, which described a number of pictures as by Giorgione, one of which was probably the *Three Philosophers* (Vienna) and another possibly, but less certainly, the *Tempest*. Even this diary dated from fifteen years and more after Giorgione's death – by which time some degree of confusion had already set in – while other famous works, such as the Castelfranco altarpiece (*Catalogue*, n.12) could be traced back no farther then the mid-seventeenth century.

But in 1931 the inscription on the back of the small portrait called *Laura* (Vienna; n.13) was first published in facsimile and discussed, and this, giving a precise attribution (which seemed absolutely contemporary) to Giorgione, as well as a date – 1506 – provided at last a solid foundation for style criticism. Every one of the characteristics of the *Laura* was now studied attentively – the crisp touch, whereby the highlights were added to the leaves round the lady's head, the angle of the face, the rich contrasts of colour and texture. Above all, the small scale. The hard core which now emerged as generally acceptable and accepted – the *Three Philosophers*, the *Tempest*, the *Laura* itself, the Berlin *Boy*, the Washington *Nativity* and *Holy Family*, the National Gallery *Adoration*, and, on a slightly larger, but still not large scale, the Leningrad *Judith* and the Castelfranco altarpiece – now seemed to show a considerable homogeneity. A few others such as the so-called *Tramonto* (National Gallery) – which was not discovered until shortly after the publication of the *Laura* inscription – now muscled in, among them the portrait of a hideous old woman inscribed *Col Tempo* (Venice, Accademia; n. 20) which Berenson, fancifully but brilliantly, imagined as Giorgione's warning to the young lady of the *Tempest* (so similar in cast of countenance) of what old age would do to her – particularly if she continued to reject his advances.

The problem now shifted. If the authorship of pictures such as these was now more or less established on the strength of the *Laura* inscription they must also be linked with it to some extent as regards date – 1506. And Giorgione still had another four years of life after this. What did he do with them? There were official contracts, but we are in no position to judge the result. In one case – the frescoes on the Fondaco dei Tedeschi in Venice (1508) – Giorgione's work has perished except for a ruined fragment. Of the other – a picture for the Doge's Palace (1507–8) – nothing definite is known, though it has been suggested that Giorgione's picture may be the *Judgement of Solomon*, now at Kingston Lacy. What would Giorgione's style have been like at this stage of his life? Here a most revealing remark dropped by Vasari in his life of Titian seemed to give a clue. According to this, it was "about the year 1507" that Giorgione remodelled his style from a dry to a broader method of painting. From this alone we might expect that the "later" Giorgione would fade almost imperceptibly into the earlier style of Titian and others, and such is likely to have been the case. The resulting confusion needs no emphasis, and has been greatly increased by the implications of statements by several of the early writers, to the effect

that certain pictures which Giorgione had left unfinished at his death were completed by Titian or by the young Sebastiano del Piombo. In this category are probably the Dresden *Venus,* perhaps (but in that case only minimally) the *Three Philosophers,* perhaps the *Fête Champêtre* (Louvre; n. 35) and perhaps the high altar of S. Giovanni Crisostomo, Venice. With the exception of the *Venus,* the line of demarcation in these works, if it exists at all, is almost inscrutable, so the "later" Giorgione – that is, his output between 1506 and 1510 – is still in dispute.

The fact that in the surviving documents Giorgione is described as a native of Castelfranco, that as early as 1506 (the earliest documentary reference) he was evidently settled in Venice, where he enjoyed a brief period of success, and where he died, four years later, gives at least an outline of a career. The accident of talent – of genius, even – happening to a provincial youth is enough to explain the change of residence. By a certain date the modest resources of the city of Castelfranco – some twenty-five miles from Venice – were no longer sufficient to contain the aspirations of the young artist. And though it would be possible that the Castelfranco altar was sent back there from Venice it would be more likely to have been painted while Giorgione was still living there and could get local credit from it, and therefore to represent his "early" manner – distinct both from the undefined "late" style and from the "middle period", namely the pictures grouped round the *Laura* of 1506.

The picture (n. 12) is already strikingly original when compared with works which preceded it – by Cima or even Giovanni Bellini himself. The figures in it do not "overlap" at all. They are much smaller in relation to the size of the picture than was normal. The standing saints are thus farther from each other and the Madonna entirely above both of them. The object of this was evidently to leave more space for the landscape background – a strange and illogical feature, in any case, to include behind a throne, but destined to be the cardinal element in the Giorgionesque repertory. The interplay of figures and landscape, with the two co-ordinated rather than with one subordinate to the other, was to be Giorgione's permanent theme, and that of the early Titian, the early Sebastiano, Palma Vecchio and the others who followed them.

In the Castelfranco altarpiece, as indeed in any formal work, such an interest could hardly find its fullest expression, and it is surprising that Giorgione was able to infuse as much of his novelty into it as he did. But in smaller and more informal pictures, such as the *Three Philosophers* or the *Tempest*, Giorgione's poetic vein had full scope. Characteristically, we are not sure of the subject in either case. Vasari went so far as to suggest that Giorgione's frescoes on the Fondaco dei Tedeschi represented no subject, and even if he were wrong, the fact that he, a near-contemporary, was unable to tell what it was amounts to much the same thing. So with the *Three Philosophers* and the *Tempest* the painter seems content to use the totality of the figures and the landscape to express a mood, a dream state, where his imagination and his sensibility could create things of timeless beauty unhampered by considerations of precise illustration.

For the controversial final phase, the Dresden *Venus* – though its documentary authenticity is more than shaky – is perhaps a safer guide than the other candidates. It probably *is* the picture which Giorgione is said to have started and in which Titian is said to have finished the landscape and the Cupid (the remains of the latter were uncovered in the nineteenth century and then painted over again). The more insistent mystery of the *Tempest* is no longer present, and the prominence of the landscape, at least in the picture's present state, has been reduced in favour of the dominance of the figure (we may well wonder, though, if this was not Titian's doing also: did he perhaps cut down some of the area reserved by Giorgione for the landscape?)

Despite the increased grandeur of the result – when compared with the informality of the *Tempest* – the *Venus* retains an impression of the mysterious for reasons which are difficult to pin down. The theme, though less fantastic than that of the *Tempest*, is still decidedly dream-like – the dream of every young man of finding a beautiful girl naked, asleep and unprotected. But something in the pose, relaxed but completely confident, communicates the idea of a goddess and not just of an ordinary mortal. To test this we have only to compare her with Manet's *Olympia* (Louvre) who is shown in the same pose. And even Titian's so-called *Venus of Urbino* (Uffizi) of only a few decades later, is already half way to mortality.

In default of a sufficient body of authentic works of Giorgione's last years we may most easily gauge his impact by studying the work of his immediate followers. One of the closest of them, it is true – Sebastiano del Piombo – defaulted to Rome soon after Giorgione's death and changed his style when he got there. But Palma Vecchio continued in the Giorgionesque manner throughout his career, and it indelibly marked the sixty glorious years of worldly success which Titian was to enjoy after Giorgione's death. Though his style underwent repeated modifications and transformations, and ended, at least as regards his method of handling pigment, totally unrecognisable from that of his beginnings, Titian always retained a fondness for the theme of figures romantically setting off, and set off by, a lyrical landscape. And through him – more of necessity than directly through Giorgione's own few surviving pictures – something of the Giorgionesque tradition was handed down to Poussin and Rubens and other disparate talents in the seventeenth century, to Watteau and to innumerable painters of the Picturesque in the eighteenth, and to Manet, Cézanne and others within a century of our own time.

Cecil Gould

7

# An outline of the artist's critical history

Facts concerning Giorgione's biography, his artistic development, his followers and even his imitators are intimately connected, both with each other and with the growing or decrease of his renown. We have dealt separately with the above subjects but we must also make a comprehensive survey in order not to confuse by repetition and cross references the unwieldly panoramic view of the master's art. Such an essay is given in an introduction to the *Catalogue* of Giorgione's works (pages 85–86).

Leonardo da Vinci, Mantegna, Raphael, Michelangelo and Georgio da Castelfranco are all most excellent painters, yet they are very unlike each other in their style. No one of them revealed any lack of quality in the work he achieved, for everybody knows each was perfect in his own way.

B. Castiglione, Il cortegiano, 1528

... Giorgio da Castelfranco ... a highly esteemed painter ... and he is as worthy of honor as are the ancient masters.

P. Pino, Dialogo di pittura, 1548

... Giorgio da Castelfranco ... a highly esteemed painter ... by whom are seen certain very lively oil paintings with contours so gradually fading into the background that no shadows are apparent.

L. Dolce, Dialogo della pittura, 1557

Giorgione had seen some things by the hand of Leonardo da Vinci with delicately blended colours and contours heavily darkened by shadows as has been said. This manner pleased him so much that, as long as he lived, he always pursued it and imitated it in his oil paintings. As he took much pleasure in good work, he always chose the most beautiful and varied objects he could find. Nature gave him such a sweet disposition that in his oil paintings and frescoes he made both very lively things and others which were soft and harmonious with carefully blended shadows, so that many of the excellent masters of the time confessed that he had been born to put life into figures and to counterfeit the freshness of living flesh better than any other painter, not only in Venice, but throughout the world.
... by about 1507, Giorgione da Castelfranco had begun to show a greater softness and depth in his work in a wonderful manner, while at the same time portraying living and natural things, by counterfeiting skilfully with colour and by painting sharp and soft shadows as the living thing showed. He made no drawings for he firmly believed that the best and true way of creating a picture was by painting alone and by the use of colour. He did not realise that he who wishes to arrange the various elements of a composition and develop the invention should first make many different sketches on paper in order to be able to judge the whole.

G. Vasari, Le vite, 1568[2]

At the same time that Leonardo was bringing fame to Florence, Giorgione da Castel Franco in the district of Treviso, being equal in excellence, was making the name of Venice famous. He was brought up in Venice and devoted himself with so much concentration to art that in painting he surpassed Giovanni and Gentile Bellini and gave such vitality to his figures that they seemed to live.

[2]R. Borghini, Il Riposo, 1584

Giorgione da Castelfranco was most skilful in painting fish in clear water, trees and fruit and anything he wished with the most marvellous art.

G. P. Lomazzo, Trattato dell' arte della pittura, 1584

Giorgione, you were the first to learn how to create marvels in painting; and as long as the world and mankind exist your name will be on men's lips.
Until your time other painters have made statues, whereas you have fashioned living beings and have infused them with life by your colours.
I do not say that Leonardo is not the God of Tuscany: but Giorgione also walks the Venetian path to eternal glory.

M. Boschini, La carta del navegar pitoresco, 1660

In painting he used soft brush strokes such as were unknown in the past: and one must confess that in his painting he created the illusion of flesh and blood; but with an easy, mellow touch so that one can hardly speak of pictorial counterfeit but of natural truth; because in blurring the contours (even Nature can dazzle) in placing light and half-shadows, in the reds, in lessening and increasing the strength of the colours he created such a charming and true harmony that one must call his work painted Nature or naturalised painting. The ideas of this Painter are all solemn, majestic and worthy of respect, in keeping indeed with his name – Giorgione, and that is why his genius turned towards solemn figures wearing caps ornamented with strange plumes, dressed as in the past with shirts showing beneath their tunics and those sleeves puffing out from slits, breeches in the style of Giovanni Bellini, but of better cut: the materials of silk, velvet, damask and satins striped with wide bands; other figures wear suits of armour polished like mirrors. This was the true conception of human actions.

M. Boschini, Le ricche minere della pittura veneziana, 1674

Everyone knows that Giorgio, or Giorgione da Castelfranco, was the first amongst us to liberate painting from the restrictions prevailing in his day. He gave it the genuine character of art. By allowing genius free play he departed from the narrow track of simple reason, which governs only science; he added to solid knowledge, arbitrary caprice and fantasy in order to delight and charm. No sooner had he mastered the first principles than he began to be aware of the greatness of his own genius, which being full of fire and a certain natural violence, enabled him to soar above early timidity and to give life to painted figures which had lacked it in the past. In his hands colour acquired a subtlety which was admirably suited to portraying the bloom of living flesh. He gave to what he painted a new roundness and strength; and through the liveliness of his spirit he achieved a skill which had not been seen in painting before . . . He gave light to shadows which in reality appear rather sharp and above all he knew how to use dark masses, sometimes most ingeniously giving them more intensity than in nature; and sometimes making them softer and more cheerful by blurring the contours so that the areas formed by the masses were visible and yet not visible. Thus everyone could see the greatness of his style although what caused it was understood by few.

A. M. ZANETTI, *Della pittura veneziana*, 1771

From the time when he was a pupil of Bellini, guided by the awareness of his powers, he scorned preoccupation with petty detail and substituted for it a certain freedom, a studied carelessness, which is the essence of art and of which he can be called the inventor: no one before him had known that manner of handling the brush, so resolute, so deft in conveying an impression, so skilful in painting [things] in the distance.
He continued to develop his style by amplifying his contours, by introducing new perspectives, and livelier ideas in facial expression and gesture, by more carefully chosen drapery and other accessories, by softer and more natural gradations from one shade to another and finally by giving much more effect by chiaroscuro.

L. LANZI, *Storia pittorica della Italia*, 1795–6

Giorgione was certainly a great painter and even one of the greatest that the Renaissance produced; and yet one cannot deny that there is a certain kind of greatness that eluded him: ideal asceticism had no appeal for him . . . but outside this field he was the shaper of a revolution which embraced all branches of art and he gave an unmistakable character to all that came from his vigorous brush.

A. F. RIO, *De l'art chrétien*, 1841

There seems reason for supposing that Giorgione was the first of the modern Venetians to follow the footsteps of Bellini, and give importance to landscapes. If we believe traditions which live to our day, there was no one like him at the close of the 15th century for producing park scenery, no one who came near him in the chastened elegance of the figures with which this scenery was enlivened. The country which he knew had not the rocky character nor had it the giddy heights of that which Titian found at Cadore. It had no dolomites to spread their jagged edges on the pure horizon: but it had its elms and cypresses, its vines and mulberries, its hazels and poplars, its charming undulations,

wooded vales, farm buildings and battlements; and in these there was a variety which all but defied repetition.

J. A. CROWE – G. B. CAVALCASELLE, *A History of Painting in North Italy*, 1871

. . . He is the inventor of *genre*, of those easily movable pictures which serve neither for uses of devotion, nor for allegorical or historic teaching – little groups of real men and women, amid congruous furniture or landscape – morsels of actual life, conversation or music or play, but refined upon or idealised, till they come to seem like glimpses of life from afar . . . he is typical of that aspiration of all the arts towards music, which I have endeavoured to explain, – towards the perfect identification of matter and form.

W. PATER, *The School of Giorgione*, 1877

Giorgione did not display all his powers until the last six years of his short life, that is from 1504 until about 1511. In the few works which have come down to us . . . his original and eminently poetic genius shines with such purity, his simple and straightforward artistic disposition speaks to us so forcibly and with so much charm that no one who has ever contemplated it can ever forget it. No other painter can so easily entrance us, captivate our minds for hours together; even though often we have not the least idea of what the figures in his picture mean.

I. LERMOLIEFF (G. MORELLI), *Die Werke italienischer Meister*, 1880

Giorgione's life was short, and very few of his works – not a score in all – have escaped destruction. But these suffice to give us a glimpse into that brief moment when the Renaissance found its most genuine expression in painting. Its over-boisterous passions had quieted down into a sincere appreciation of beauty and of human relations. It would be really hard to say more about Giorgione than this, that his pictures are the perfect reflex of the Renaissance at its height.

B. BERENSON, *The Venetian Painters of the Renaissance*, 1894

I contemplate Giorgione as reigning supreme on immortal heights but I cannot recognise him as a human being; I seek him in the mystery of the fiery cloud that envelops him. He is more like a myth than a man. No poet's destiny can be compared with his. All, or almost all, about him is unknown; and some have even denied that he ever lived. His name is written on no work and no work is attributed to him with certainty. Yet the whole of Venetian art seems to have caught fire from his revelation. The great Titian himself appears to have received from him the secret of infusing a stream of luminous blood into the veins of the beings he creates.

G. D'ANNUNZIO, *Il fuoco*, 1898

At a period when there was perfect harmony in the expression of religious ideals between faith and naturalistic observation, he brought about a realistic revolution by enlarging the circle of his observation, by concentrating on nature the love inherent in him, and by his eagerness for life.
Therefore he brought to the interpretation of reality elements which had escaped the most acute observers, because he looked down from a world of fantasy and from this altitude he was able to embrace with his glance a vaster horizon. He did not descend and lose himself in reality, nor did he remain shut in in a fantasy

world: his spirit continued to hover between the necessity of raising nature to his own height and the necessity of abandoning himself to nature. Hence a two-fold achievement of realistic reform and the expression of a new state of mind.

. . . The penetrating and profound sensitivity of the young artist from Castelfranco enabled him to enjoy reality, to study it, to interpret it, to surrender himself to the joy of living. For a short time. Then he felt compelled to make spirit apparent and to return to the religious abandons. The strength of religious sentiment having grown weak, cultivated men turned to scepticism. Giorgione could not return to the past, nor could he adapt himself to the present; and not knowing how to give shape to the new conceptions he confined himself to creating dreams full of nostalgia for that which could no longer be found.

A balance between the new and the old was beyond his power as an artist, but his desire to achieve it was keen, almost morbid. In this resides the fascination of his art.

L. VENTURI, *Giorgione e il giorgionismo*, 1913

The uncertainty of his craftsmanship is a further proof of how little Giorgione owes to the Venetian school. Even in the Castelfranco altarpiece, whose three figures, in spite of everything derive from Bellini's iconographical material, Giorgione's faces and drapery are those of an artist who, through ignorance or contempt, chooses to lose himself in his own innovations rather than follow the beaten track. A face, a fold, a hand, present difficulties which an ordinary craftsman learnt to overcome: but it is not certain that Giorgione can be described as such a craftsman. Except in some problems for which he had found the solution – a rock, foliage and above all some feminine faces – Giorgione reveals a technique more curious than strictly accurate. His weaknesses give him the reputation of being independent, and this has certainly done him no harm in the eyes of the moderns.

There are two motifs in which clearly he seems to have been an innovator: in landscape and nudes, and in the relation of nudes and landscape. The most beautiful of all his landscapes is that showing a new and convincing vision of the Castelfranco walls growing pale in the light of a thunderstorm. The artist who was capable of conveying such an impression is one of those painter-poets who have added the beauty of painting to the poetry of nature.

L. HOURTICQ, *Le problème de Giorgione*, 1930

Giorgione is the spring-time of Venetian art and of world painting; his is the important mastery of colour as an essential means of expression, he is the whole of painting, both heaven and earth; in him art, having come to maturity through almost a century of experience, has become self-conscious. Having outgrown Bellini's pedantry and mastered and improved painting in the best Antonello tradition, even the background, until then the inert spectator of pictorial events previously devoted to figures and landscape, becomes atmosphere; that is to say one of the essential components of painting; an element in the artistic drama, of the same importance as any other. All the components of the picture have their position; those significant components which are at the base of our expression and our sensibility.

G. FIOCCO, *Giorgione*, 1941

Whatever may be the precise theme of the picture *The Tempest*, the impression it gives us is this: it causes man to become part of nature, makes him vibrate with it, become one with it or lose himself in it, according to a concept of the return to nature which is the basis of modern art. And as these words are here expressed in painting for the first time with the virginal fragrance of ideas flowering from the souls of poets, the power of suggestion of such a work is absolute.

The *Tempest* is Giorgione's most personal work, the one best expressing his state of mind when confronted with nature; not only because of the unusual pictorial concept which has seemed so mysterious, but also for the treatment of the pictorial matter. In this picture outlines are dissolved in every movement, they adapt themselves to the fantasy of the artist and to the reality of nature transfigured by that fantasy; there is a continual vibration of lines, not understood as contours but as waves in motion, achieved by the adaptation of tone with tone, by the liquidity of the chosen range of colours – from yellow ochre to light red, from pale green to dark blue and deep emerald . . .

A. MORASSI, *Giorgione*, 1942

The art of Giorgione is certainly complex in its development, its aesthetic interests and its cultural values, so much so that from its first appearance it gave rise to many and contradictory figurative interpretations and to a multiplicity of reactions in the field of art history. Giorgione's style is not so exclusive in character as that of Tintoretto or Carpaccio: from a nucleus of inspiration narrowly confined by colour and light, that is to say the tone of the picture, spring ever new outbursts of fantasy spreading over different planes. Giorgione's cultural alertness, his lively participation in all the interests of his day, possesses the gift, proper to genius, of transforming itself by a purely imaginative and lyrical process into a perfect work of art. The practical result of his naturally responsive sensitivity is to sever the chains of fifteenth-century traditional iconography, whether religious or profane. A new mythology of figurative representation is born with Giorgione in which man is in contact with nature in such a way that the latter sometimes dares to assume the role of protagonist; a new dignity enriches the psychology of his human beings who, in their isolation, are invested with a new profundity . . . The revolution he brought about in the world of art lay not only in the transformation of objects but in a complete renewal of figurative sensibility.

R. PALLUCCHINI, *La pittura veneziana del Cinquecento*, 1944

. . . Having introduced in the *Three Philosophers* and the Donà dalle Rose *Tramonto* . . . the first accents of chromatic classicism, soon after to be developed by the young Titian, Giorgione gives himself up to painting his half-length figures in colour without making any preliminary sketches and creates the sensual naturalism in his portraits which gives an impression of action, as in the *Self-Portrait as David*, the *Warrior whose Page is Buckling on his Armour* and similar portraits which must have existed and belonged to the last months of his life. These were almost modern works, approaching Caravaggio, Velázquez and Manet.

R. LONGHI, *Viatico per cinque secoli di pittura veneziana*, 1946

. . . When one remembers that almost all Giorgione's work was carried out in less than ten years, the marvellous difference between purpose and technique seems all the greater.

It is for this reason that modern criticism has tried to attribute several of his pictures to different artists: Titian, Sebastiano del Piombo, Palma and others who are nameless. The attribution to Titian of late works by Giorgione can be upheld on purely technical grounds but not on those of expression. Sebastiano del Piombo and Palma must be excluded on the same grounds and with greater justification. We are too familiar with the activity of Venetian painters at the beginning of the sixteenth century to suppose a nameless artist capable of creating pictures of such worth as those attributed to Giorgione.

It only remains to say that the diversity in Giorgione's work is inherent in his style. Starting from the taste of masters such as Bellini and Carpaccio he proceeded uncertainly in several directions, both towards linear purity and a painterly touch, covering as much ground in a few years as had Venetian painting in a century, experimenting with everything from time to time except his way of feeling which is constant. One cannot say that Giorgione was more a poet than a painter, only that, because he was more of a poet than other artists, he created a new pictorial civilisation and a new vision of the world. Nor is it surprising that a young man between twenty-five and thirty, in achieving this miracle, should have had moments of uncertainty, of feeling thrown in on himself, of sudden moods and of weariness.

Only by discarding traditional ways of stylistic criticism can one reach any understanding of Giorgione's personality and realise how he learnt from Leonardo, perhaps from Raphael, and, at the same time, from Hieronymus Bosch; and had shared in the philosophical culture of his day and in the manner of feeling nature expressed by such poets as Giovanni Pontano, Giovanni Cotta and Jacopo Sannazzaro.

L. Venturi, Giorgione, 1954

That intimate concentration on individual figures, that suspension of all movement, that silence, all are expressions of Giorgione's feeling in contrast to Titian's. The latter exuberant artist in his early work searches for movement, eloquent gestures, models from ordinary people, over-elaborate drapery, the play of light – if not from other sources – from passing clouds, and crowded compositions . . . With Giorgione calm reigns, spiritual concentration, a sense of space, the harmony of rich and intense colours.

C. Gamba, Il mio Giorgione in "Arte Veneta", 1954

The secret of Giorgione – to which so much mystery and secrets are attributed – is simply that he saw the whole spectacle of the world as a "non-tangible", but exclusively "visible distance", and he reduced all representation to "pure colour". Painting then becomes genuinely and exclusively "painting"; that is to say it gives up all claim to emulate or simulate sculpture or, worse still, to offer an equivalent, rather than an image, of reality; it thus overcomes the ambiguity of Renaissance artists in regard to the illusive imitation of nature. Colour and movement have some value for them (Vasari emphasised the skill in conveying by painting almost the breath of life and the warmth of flesh) but their principal objective is still a three-dimensional representation.

L. Coletti, Giorgione, 1955

. . . In this important work [the Castelfranco altarpiece], youthful freshness of invention is allied to important figurative novelties. Immersed in the vibrant atmosphere of nature, not designed as a perspective decoration as in fifteenth-century paintings but existing as coloured space, the figures move with the sureness foreshadowing the development from the *Three Philosophers* to the frescoes of the Fondaco dei Tedeschi. Colour in this new movement of forms naturally dominates. But it is no longer understood as filling in the superficial limits imposed by contours and plastic planes, but spreads in a new spatiality, having the same characteristics as the free verse of the sixteenth century. What had been a premature discovery by Giovanni Bellini and Antonello, and perhaps above all by Carpaccio – that is, the atmospheric value of colour understood in its continual tonal variations – becomes the means of expression in Giorgione's style in the Castelfranco altarpiece.

This is his extraordinary fascination, like a base melody of musical chords, overcoming all fifteenth-century grammar which, henceforward, seemed conventional even to those who invented it.

T. Pignatti, Giorgione, 1955

Entrance without fear or hindrance into the world of nature and the world of human spirit; his approach, I might almost say abandonment, to a contemplative vision of the whole universe, this is Giorgione's achievement. That he portrayed this world in pictures vibrant with light, trembling and alive, is the painter's second gift to us. To answer the question, therefore, as to whether Giorgione be truly great, as his contemporaries had known instinctively and as has always been accepted, one must say that he is even greater than has always been held. It is true that his works are few, and some are uncertain as to their authorship; and it is true that discussions about them will continue and will go on perhaps for ever. But one thing is certain: he has thrown open doors on to a pictorial world which is more completely ours.

P. Zampetti, Postille alla mostra di Giorgione, in "Arte Veneta", 1955

. . . What we can try to reconstruct in this final example of Giorgione's art [the *Nude* from the Fondaco dei Tedeschi in the Accademia in Venice], is decisive not only for the last phase of his painting but for the influence he had in and beyond his lifetime. It is the logical consequence of the ground he wished to cover, of his lofty vision of an artist's ideal, even if it appeared to his contemporaries as "novel". In this sense the fragment in the Accademia is more than a proof. It constitutes the certainty that a break came in tradition and that a decisive turn was given towards the conquest of modern art. With the sureness of genius Giorgione resolved in the "grand manner" the most serious of his problems which he shared with Michelangelo: the vision of man dominating nature, even if man, in his turn, is the prisoner of a destiny full of sorrow.

P. Della Pergola, Giorgione, 1957

Very often an effort is made to see in Giorgione's paintings the development of a story which in reality does not exist or is merely put in as a pretext . . . The truth is that Giorgione's art shows that decrease in the importance of the subject in favour of artistic expression which anticipates modern art.

L. Venturi, Giorgione, in "Enciclopedia Universale dell'Arte", VII, 1958

# Note on the Giorgionesque

Here are some brief notes on painters who, at least for a time, worked in Giorgione's style (some works by them have been attributed to the master, as is shown in the *Catalogue*). There were certainly other artists as well whose names have remained unknown.

PARIS BORDONE (Treviso, 1500 – Venice, 1571). Probably a pupil of Titian's but much influenced by Giorgione's example even after the first half of the century. Among his most significant and justly well-known works is the so-called *Venetian Lovers* in the Brera Gallery in Milan, where – as in some portraits – a mysterious and melancholy atmosphere predominates, an intimate tone, fully in accord with that of the master.

GIOVANNI BUSI called CARIANI (Venice, 1480–1490 – some documents refer to him after 1547). If in early works such as the *Madonna and St Sebastian* in the Louvre he seems to borrow directly from Giovanni Bellini, and in other respects to resemble Palma Vecchio, he later shows himself influenced above all by Giorgione. Thus, in the *Lovers* in the Palazzo Venezia in Rome he takes up the theme of the *Fête Champêtre* (n. 35); and he appears even more noticeably Giorgionesque in the *Lute Player*, one of his more psychologically penetrating portraits, in the Musée des Beaux-Arts in Strasbourg, in which his stylistic resemblance to Giorgione is almost complete.

GIULIO CAMPAGNOLA (Padua, 1482–1515?). A painter, but better known as an engraver, to whom we owe the discovery of the "pricking" technique (the so-called *pointillée au maillet*), by which atmospheric tonal nuances similar to those obtained by Giorgione in painting can be transferred on to a metal plate. Having been brought up in Padua in Mantegna's circle and having moved to Venice in 1507, he must have been strongly attracted to the style introduced by Giorgione. This is shown by the manner in which Campagnola painted the three *Stories of the Madonna* in the Paduan Scuola del Carmine or the *Youth Playing a Musical Instrument* in the Thyssen Collection in Lugano. But it is in Campagnola's engravings that Giorgione's influence is most apparent, and in these it determined not only his technique but his choice of subject.

VINCENZO CATENA (Venetian?, documented from 1495 to 1531). At first he reacted to Giovanni Bellini and Cima da Conegliano; then to Giorgione who became his friend and collaborator (the inscription on the reverse of *Laura* in Vienna [*Catalogue*, n. 13] suggests this). He followed Giorgione closely for a considerable time, from his *Judith* in the Querini Stampalia Foundation in Venice (1500–1502) to the *Martyrdom of St Christina* in the same city (1520).

GIAMBATTISTA CIMA called CIMA DA CONEGLIANO (Conegliano Veneto, c. 1459 – Venice, c. 1518). From his master, Bartolomeo Montagna, he acquired the gift of clear luminous modelling as seen in the *Madonna della Pergola* in the Museo Civico of Vicenza (1489); then, working in Venice from 1492, he turned his attention to Antonello da Messina and Giovanni Bellini, to whom he owed a more softly integrated chromatic texture and the more balanced compositions in which he portrayed visions permeated with genuine classicism. In paintings such as the *Madonna and Child* in the Rijksmuseum of Amsterdam, or in the oval paintings *Endymion Asleep* and *Apollo and Marsyas* in the National Gallery of Parma he reveals affinities with Giorgione. These are clear although difficult to explain in the sense that one cannot be certain whether Giorgione influenced his young colleague, as Coletti thinks, or whether it was the other way round.

BERNARDINO LICINIO (Poscante [Bergamo]?, c. 1489 – Venice, c. 1565). When still young he went to Venice and fell under the spell of its painters, in particular Giorgione and Palma Vecchio. One is conscious of the former's influence above all in the presumed *Portrait of Ettore Fieramosca* (Museo Civico, Vicenza), attributed for a long time to the master himself; while in allegories of classical type, such as that in the Kress Foundation of New York, he shows Palma's influence. Towards the end of his life his manner hardened and he expressed himself consistently in heavy, dead colours, as in the *Madonna* in the Frari in Venice.

SEBASTIANO LUCIANI called SEBASTIANO VENEZIANO and SEBASTIANO DEL PIOMBO (Venice, c. 1485 – Rome, 1547). In his youth, with his companion Titian, he was very close to Giorgione, so much so that works begun by the master and left unfinished at his death were entrusted to him and also to Titian to be finished. This was the case – according to Michiel – with the *Three Philosophers* now in Vienna (n. 17). In regard to the altarpiece in S. Giovanni Crisostomo in Venice (c. 1509) Vasari states that the figures of the saints "had in them so much of Giorgione's manner that they were often taken to be by Giorgione himself".

GIOVANNI LUTERI called DOSSO DOSSI (Ferrara, c. 1479 – c. 1542). In all probability a pupil of his fellow citizen Lorenzo Costa, he formed himself on the study of Venetian paintings. He was probably familiar with those of Titian while working in Mantua in 1512 and with those of Giorgione (Titian himself may have suggested that he study Giorgione's work) when from 1516 he was in the service of Alfonso d'Este in Ferrara. Among his paintings most closely resembling those of the two Venetian artists the *Nymph Pursued by a Satyr* in the Pitti in Florence may be mentioned and the *Bacchanal* in the Castle of St Angelo in Rome. Later, perhaps during a visit to Rome, he was influenced by the classicism of Raphael.

LORENZO LUZZO called IL MORTO DA FELTRE (working from the end of the fifteenth century until 1527). According to Vasari he helped Giorgione with the work for the Fondaco dei Tedeschi (1508): certainly he shows contacts (not necessarily direct) with a Giorgionesque idiom in the altarpiece now in Berlin (Staatliche Museen), in a work in the parish church of Villabruna, and in the *Apparition of Christ to Two Saints* in the Ognissanti church in Feltre, although in the latter the greater breadth in the forms and in the chromatic texture reveals a keen interest in Raphael's painting.

DOMENICO MANCINI (from Treviso?, first half of the sixteenth century). From a documentary point of view he is known exclusively in connection with a painting signed and dated 1511, and evidently derived from Giovanni Bellini – the *Madonna* in the Duomo at Lendinara. In other paintings, such as the *Music Player* in the Kunsthistorisches Museum in Vienna or the *Two Young Men* in the Palazzo Venezia in Rome, he seems to be a very close follower of Giorgione.

"MASTER OF THE SELF-PORTRAITS". Wilde [1933] says he is

the author of pictures such as the *Musician* in the Kunsthistorisches Museum in Vienna, but this is more likely to be by Domenico Mancini in his most Giorgionesque phase; Wilde thinks, however, that the "Master of the Self-Portraits" might be identified with a certain Domenico da Venezia, who is distinct from Mancini.

"MASTER OF THE IDYLLS". According to Wilde [1933], he is the author of works such as the *Lovers* in the Palazzo Venezia in Rome, but this is more likely to be by Cariani at his most Giorgionesque. Wilde thinks that this unknown painter could perhaps be Mancini.

PIETRO MUTTONI called PIETRO VECCHIA or DELLA (DALLA) VECCHIA (Venice, 1603–1678). He owes this curious name to his cleverness in imitating old pictures. It is said that he arranged for the cleaning, among other paintings, of Giorgione's altarpiece at Castelfranco (n. 12). It is worthwhile giving the following quotation from Boschini [1664]: "To the glory of Giorgione and of Pietro Vecchia, a contemporary Venetian painter, and to the intelligent understanding of amateurs, I must say that they should have their eye on this Vecchia because they will recognise work from his brush transformed into Giorgionesque forms so that it is impossible to tell whether it was painted by Giorgione or is an imitation by Vecchia, and even many of the most knowledgeable have gathered fruit from the latter imagining that it came from the other tree." In fact Muttoni's activity has contributed not a little to causing misunderstandings and errors about Giorgione's work, because copies and imitations by the seventeenth-century painter were ascribed to him.

IACOPO NEGRETTI called PALMA IL VECCHIO (Serina [Bergamo], *c.* 1480 – Venice, 1528). By 1510 he was already known in Venice in the circle surrounding Giorgione. But the Giorgionesque influence was not confined to his youth; it is even more strongly reflected in the deeper serenity and the placid opulence of the *Sacre Conversazioni* and also in the two *Portraits of the Querini* (Querini Stampalia Foundation, Venice), which were amongst his last works.

GEROLAMO DA ROMANO called ROMANINO (Brescia, *c.* 1484 – 1566?). Giorgione's ascendancy over him was a youthful episode in his complicated artistic development and grafted on to the deep Lombard culture that profoundly affected his huge altarpiece in the Museo Civico in Padua. Giorgione's influence grew less, without ever quite disappearing; it is just perceptible in the frescoes in the Castello del Buonconsiglio at Trent (1531–2).

GIOVANNI ANTONIO DE' SACCHIS (or DE' LODESANIS) called PORDENONE(or REGILLO) (Pordenone, *c.* 1483 – Ferrara, 1539). In 1508, in Ferrara, he collaborated with Pellegrino da S. Daniele; then he worked in Rome and fell under the spell of Raphael, whose work inspired his magniloquent but robust plasticism in the work he did for the Duomo at Treviso (1520) and for the Duomo at Cremona; later, however, in his frescoes in the church of the Madonna di Campagna in Piacenza (1531–6) and in Venice, his Roman dynamism was to show itself receptive to the elegance of the Mannerists of Parma, and Tintoretto's early work was to be conditioned by them. Pordenone showed an independent spirit and almost always succeeded in translating into personal terms the idea by which he was influenced. This applies to his relations with Giorgione. He was much influenced by him during his youth but transformed Giorgione's use of colour into the very full-bodied chromatic intensity seen in works such as his altarpiece for the Duomo in his native city.

GIAN GEROLAMO SAVOLDO (Brescia, *c.* 1480 – after 1548). He may have been a pupil of Bonsignori and influenced by Giovanni Bellini and others – Jan van Scorel and Palma Vecchio among them – ; yet Giorgione's example was the most important factor in his early work and for a great part of his artistic career. The themes, the vision – in a word, Savoldo's world – derive without doubt from Giorgione; but he expresses them by working up the light and shadow into elaborate contrasts, thus creating a subtly poetic atmosphere. Among his paintings most influenced by Giorgione are *Gaston de Foix* in the Louvre, the *Young Peasant* and the *Flute Player* in the Contini Bonacossi Collection in Florence, in the second of which one recognises a touch of Lorenzo Lotto's pungency of approach.

DAVID TENIERS (Antwerp, 1610 – Brussels, 1690). Painter and engraver who, in his own art, has nothing in common with the master of Castelfranco, being orientated towards Rubens and, above all, Brouwer; nevertheless he is of some importance to Giorgione studies because after the Archduke Leopold William appointed him his personal painter (1647), he supervised the engraving of the Italian pictures collected by his patron in the well-known *Theatrum Pictorium*. Through these engravings, examples of Giorgione's work – or of work attributed to him such as the *David* or the *Bravo* (n. 76 and 65) – have been preserved, while some copies in oils also make certain comparisons possible, as in the case of *Laura* (n. 13).

FRANCESCO TORBIDO called IL MORO (Venice, 1483–93 – Verona, 1561–2). Having learnt his craft in Verona under Liberale, he was soon attracted by Giorgione and other Venetian artists: not deeply yet not so superficially as is usually suggested. His *Young Man with a Rose* in the Bayerische Staatsgemäldesammlungen in Munich and the *Young Man with a Flageolet* in the Museo Civico of Padua give proof of this, the last for a long time attributed to Giorgione himself.

TITIAN VECELLIO (Pieve di Cadore, *c.* 1487 – Venice, 1576). After moving to Venice he was a pupil first of Gentile and then of Giovanni Bellini. In 1508 he was working at the Fondaco dei Tedeschi, in rivalry – possibly – with Giorgione, although the latter must have been in charge of the work. After Giorgione's death he completed some of his pictures such as the Dresden *Venus* (n. 21). This was not without its effect on Titian, because the dramatic energy which had characterised the latter's work from the start was opposed to Giorgione's lyrical and poetic spirit, so that Vasari attributes first to one painter and then to the other the *Christ Bearing the Cross* in the Scuola di S. Rocco at Venice (n. 27). Nor has modern criticism been any more confident in regard to the *Madonna and Child* in the Prado (n. 31) or the *Fête Champêtre* in the Louvre (n. 35). Titian continued to be influenced by Giorgione though with new and livelier results during a large part of 1510–20, and he did not overcome this influence until 1518 when he painted the altarpiece in the Church of the Frari in Venice.

# The paintings in colour

# List of Plates

*The captions under each reproduction show (in centimetres) the width of the actual painting, or of the detail of the painting reproduced.*

**PLATE I**     THE TRIAL OF MOSES BY FIRE   Florence, Uffizi
Whole (72 cm.)

**PLATE II**    THE TRIAL OF MOSES BY FIRE  Florence, Uffizi
Detail (38 cm.)

**PLATE III**   VARIOUS INSTRUMENTS, MEDALLIONS AND SCROLLS   Castelfranco Veneto, Casa Pellizzari
North-east wall, right-hand side (50 cm.)

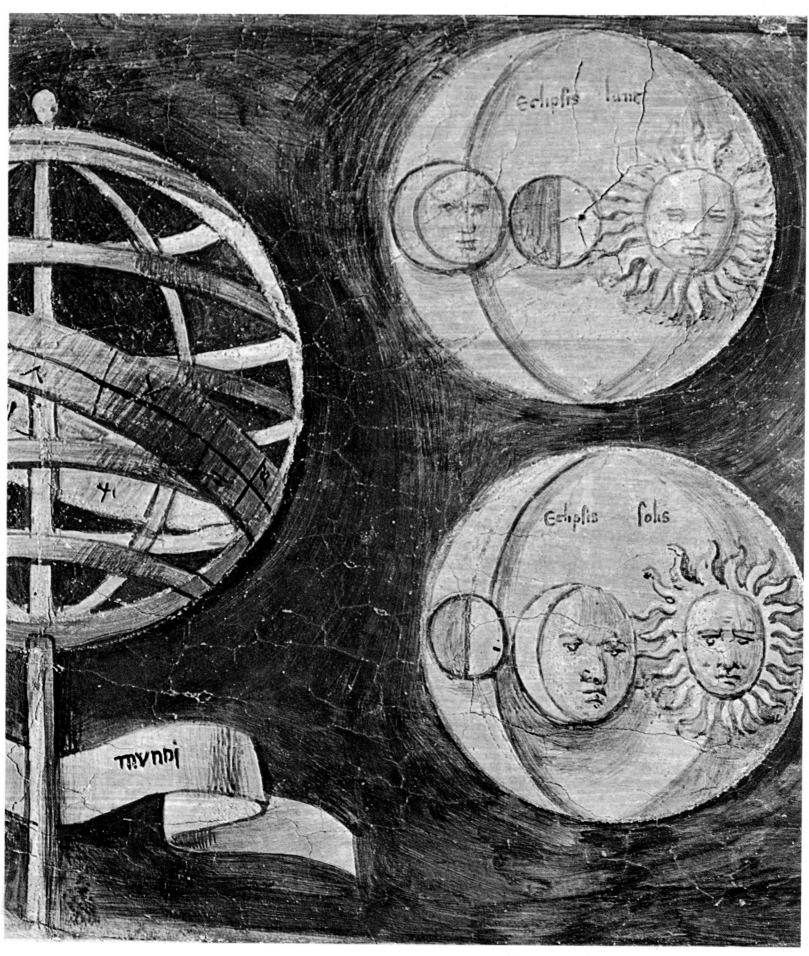

eclipfis lune

eclipfis folis

mvndi

**PLATE IV**    VARIOUS INSTRUMENTS, MEDALLIONS AND SCROLLS  Castelfranco Veneto, Casa Pellizzari
North-east wall, towards the left (50 cm.)

**PLATE V**    VARIOUS INSTRUMENTS, MEDALLIONS AND SCROLLS  Castelfranco Veneto, Casa Pellizzari
North-east wall, centre (50 cm.)

**PLATE VI**   VARIOUS INSTRUMENTS, MEDALLIONS AND SCROLLS  Castelfranco Veneto, Casa Pellizzari
North-east wall, centre, towards the right (50 cm.)

**PLATE VII**    HOLY FAMILY  Washington, National Gallery
Whole (45.5 cm.)

**PLATES VIII-IX**   THE ADORATION OF THE MAGI  London, National Gallery
Whole (81 cm.)

**PLATE X**   THE ADORATION OF THE MAGI   London, National Gallery
Detail (actual size)

**PLATE XI** THE ADORATION OF THE MAGI London, National Gallery
Detail (actual size)

**PLATE XII**   THE ADORATION OF THE MAGI   London, National Gallery
Detail (actual size)

**PLATE XIII**    THE ADORATION OF THE SHEPHERDS  Washington, National Gallery
Whole (111 cm.)

**PLATE XIV**   THE ADORATION OF THE SHEPHERDS  Washington, National Gallery
Detail (actual size)

**PLATE XV**    THE ADORATION OF THE SHEPHERDS  Washington, National Gallery
Detail (actual size)

**PLATE XVI**    THE ADORATION OF THE SHEPHERDS  Washington, National Gallery
Detail (24 cm.)

**PLATE XVII**   MADONNA READING  Oxford, Ashmolean Museum
Whole (60 cm.)

**PLATE XVIII**    MADONNA READING  Oxford, Ashmolean Museum
Detail (actual size)

**PLATE XIX**   MADONNA READING  Oxford, Ashmolean Museum
Detail (actual size)

**PLATE XX**

JUDITH  Leningrad, Hermitage
Whole (66.5 cm.)

**PLATE XXI**   ENTHRONED MADONNA AND CHILD (CASTELFRANCO ALTARPIECE)   Castelfranco Veneto, Church of S. Liberale
Whole (152 cm.)

**PLATE XXII**    ENTHRONED MADONNA AND CHILD (CASTELFRANCO ALTARPIECE)   Castelfranco Veneto, Church of S. Liberale
Detail (33 cm.)

**PLATE XXIII**    ENTHRONED MADONNA AND CHILD (CASTELFRANCO ALTARPIECE)   Castelfranco Veneto, Church of S. Liberale
Detail (24 cm.)

**PLATE XXIV**    ENTHRONED MADONNA AND CHILD (CASTELFRANCO ALTARPIECE)  Castelfranco Veneto, Church of S. Liberale
Detail (24 cm.)

**PLATE XXV**     ENTHRONED MADONNA AND CHILD (CASTELFRANCO ALTARPIECE)  Castelfranco Veneto, Church of  S. Liberale
Detail (33 cm.)

**PLATE XXVI**   ENTHRONED MADONNA AND CHILD (CASTELFRANCO ALTARPIECE)   Castelfranco Veneto, Church of S. Liberale
Detail (33 cm.)

**PLATE XXVII**  ENTHRONED MADONNA AND CHILD (CASTELFRANCO ALTARPIECE)  Castelfranco Veneto, Church of S. Liberale
Detail (41 cm.)

**PLATE XXVIII**    ENTHRONED MADONNA AND CHILD (CASTELFRANCO ALTARPIECE)  Castelfranco Veneto, Church of S. Liberale
Detail (33 cm.)

**PLATE XXIX**     ENTHRONED MADONNA AND CHILD (CASTELFRANCO ALTARPIECE)  Castelfranco Veneto, Church of S. Liberale
Detail (33 cm.)

**PLATE XXX**     PORTRAIT OF A YOUNG WOMAN (LAURA)  Vienna, Kunsthistorisches Museum
Whole (33.5 cm.)

**PLATE XXXI**     THE TEMPEST   Venice, Accademia
Whole (73 cm.)

**PLATE XXXII**     THE TEMPEST  Venice, Accademia
Detail (actual size)

**PLATE XXXIII**    THE TEMPEST  Venice, Accademia
Detail (actual size)

**PLATE XXXIV**     THE TEMPEST  Venice, Accademia
Detail (actual size)

**PLATE XXXV**    THE TEMPEST  Venice, Accademia
Detail (actual size)

**PLATES XXXVI-XXXVII**   THE TEMPEST  Venice, Accademia
Detail (actual size)

**PLATE XXXVIII**     THE TEMPEST  Venice, Accademia
Detail (actual size)

**PLATE XXXIX**    THE THREE PHILOSOPHERS  Vienna, Kunsthistorisches Museum
Whole (144.5 cm.)

**PLATE XL**    THE THREE PHILOSOPHERS  Vienna, Kunsthistorisches Museum
Detail (actual size)

**PLATE XLI**   THE THREE PHILOSOPHERS   Vienna, Kunsthistorisches Museum
Detail (actual size)

**PLATE XLII**    THE THREE PHILOSOPHERS  Vienna, Kunsthistorisches Museum
Detail (actual size)

**PLATE XLIII**   THE THREE PHILOSOPHERS   Vienna, Kunsthistorisches Museum
Detail (actual size)

**PLATES XLIV-XLV**    THE THREE PHILOSOPHERS  Vienna, Kunsthistorisches Museum
Detail (57 cm.)

**PLATE XLVI**    THE THREE PHILOSOPHERS  Vienna, Kunsthistorisches Museum
Detail (27 cm.)

**PLATE XLVII**   PORTRAIT OF AN OLD WOMAN   Venice, Accademia
Whole (59 cm.)

**PLATE XLVIII**  VIEW OF CASTELFRANCO AND A SHEPHERD  Rotterdam, Boymans-van Beuningen Museum
Whole (29 cm.)

**PLATE XLIX**     PORTRAIT OF A YOUNG MAN   Berlin, Staatliche Museen
Whole (46 cm.)

**PLATE L**  SELF-PORTRAIT  Brunswick, Herzog Anton-Ulrich-Museum
Whole (43 cm.)

**PLATE LI**   BUST OF A MAN  San Diego (California), Fine Arts Gallery
Whole (26 cm.)

**PLATES LII-LIII**     THE SLEEPING VENUS  Dresden, Gemäldegalerie
Whole (175 cm.)

**PLATE LIV**    THE SLEEPING VENUS  Dresden, Gemäldegalerie
Detail (actual size)

**PLATE LV**   THE SLEEPING VENUS  Dresden, Gemäldegalerie
Detail (actual size)

**PLATE LVI**    THE SLEEPING VENUS  Dresden, Gemäldegalerie
Detail (actual size)

**PLATE LVII**    THE SLEEPING VENUS  Dresden, Gemäldegalerie
Detail (actual size)

**PLATE LVIII**  FÊTE CHAMPÊTRE Paris, Louvre
Whole (138 cm.)

**PLATE LIX**   FÊTE CHAMPÊTRE  Paris, Louvre
Detail (actual size)

**PLATES LX-LXI**   FÊTE CHAMPÊTRE  Paris, Louvre
Detail (actual size)

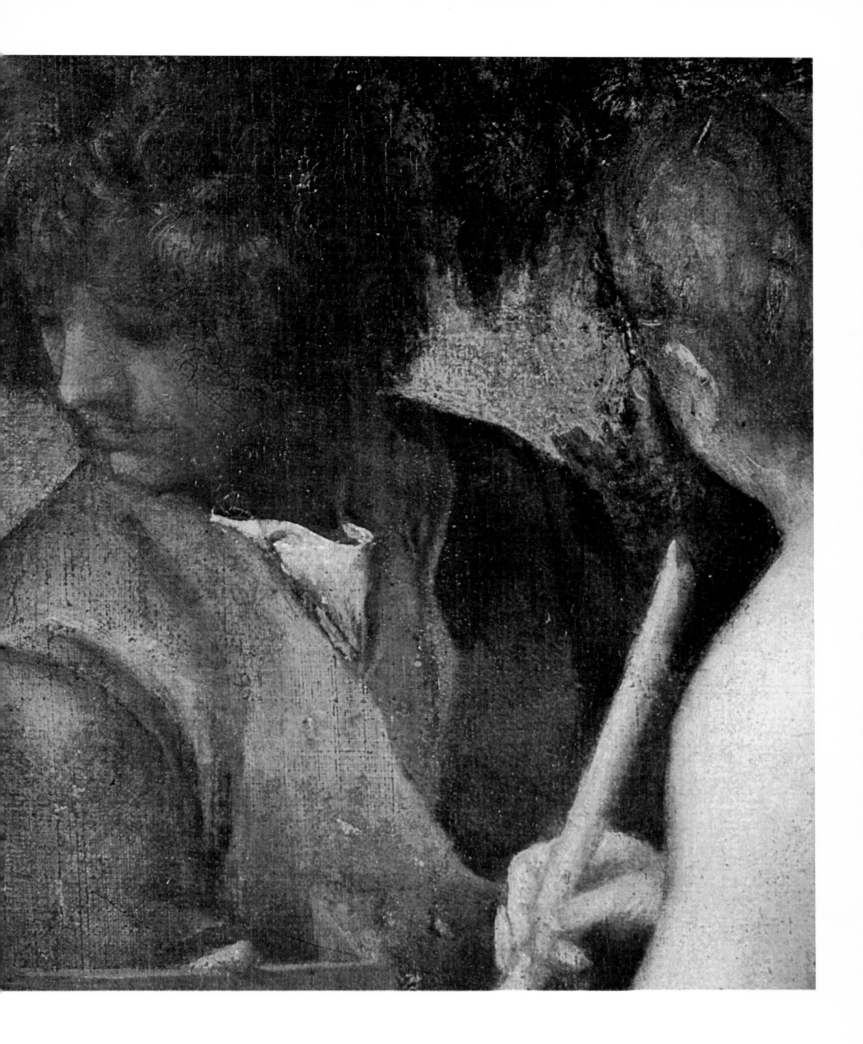

**PLATE LXII**  FÊTE CHAMPÊTRE  Paris, Louvre
Detail (27 cm.)

**PLATE LXIII**     THE THREE AGES OF MAN  Florence, Pitti Palace
Whole (77 cm.)

**PLATE LXIV**    THE THREE AGES OF MAN  Florence, Pitti Palace
Detail (actual size)

The Works

# Key to symbols used

So that the essential elements in each work may be immediately apparent, each commentary is headed first by a number (following the most reliable chronological sequence) which is given every time that the work is quoted throughout the book, and then by a series of symbols. These refer to:

1) its execution, that is, to the degree to which it is autograph,
2) its technique,
3) its support,
4) its present whereabouts.
5) The following additional data:
   whether the work is signed, dated;
   if its present-day form is complete;
   if it is a finished work.

Of the other two numbers in each heading, the upper numbers refer to the picture's measurements in centimetres (height and width); the lower numbers to its date. When the date itself cannot be given with certainty, and is therefore only approximate, it is followed or preceded by an asterisk, *, according to whether the uncertainty relates to the period before the date given, the subsequent period, or both. All the information given corresponds to the current opinion of modern art historians, any seriously different opinions and any further clarification is mentioned in the text.

### Execution

⊞ Autograph

⊞ with assistance

⊞ in collaboration

⊞ with extensive collaboration

⊞ from his workshop

⊞ currently attributed

⊞ currently rejected

▨ traditionally attributed

▨ recently attributed

### Technique

⊕ Oil

⊕ Fresco

⊕ Tempera

### Support

⊕ Wood

⊕ Plaster

⊕ Canvas

### Whereabouts

⦙ Public Collection

⦙ Private Collection

⦙ Unknown

⦙ Lost

### Additional Data

▤ Signed

▤ Dated

▤ Incomplete or fragment

▤ Unfinished

⊞⊕▤

Symbols given in the text

# Bibliography

There are very full bibliographical indexes in the monographs on Giorgione by G. M. Richter, A. Morassi and P. Della Pergola (see below). Early documentary information has been compiled from the writings of: G. VASARI [Le vite . . . ., Florence 1550, and 1568], M. A. MICHIEL [Notizie d'opere del disegno, 1525–43; ed. Morelli, 1800; ed. Frizzoni, 1884; ed. Frimmel, 1888], A. VENDRAMIN [Catalogue of the collection of Andrea Vendramin, 1627; ed. Borenius, 1923], C. RIDOLFI [Le maraviglie dell' arte. Venice 1648; ed. Hadeln, 1914], M. BOSCHINI [La carta del navegar pitoresco, Venice 1660; ed. A. Pallucchini, 1966. Le minere della pittura, Venice 1664. Le ricche minere della pittura veneziana, Venice 1674].

The most important studies are by: J. A. CROWE and G. B. CAVAL-CASELLE [A History of Painting in North Italy, London 1871], W. PATER [The School of Giorgione in the Renaissance, London 1877], I. LERMOLIEFF (G. MORELLI) [Die Werke italienischer Meister in den Galerien von München, Dresden und Berlin, Leipzig 1880. Kunst-kritische Studien über italienische Malerei. Die Galerien Borghese und Doria Panfili in Rom, Leipzig 1890], B. BERENSON [The Venetian Painters of the Renaissance, London-New York 1894. The Study and Criticism of Italian Art—1, London 1901. The Italian Painters of the Renaissance,

Oxford 1930, and later editions until that of 1957. "AV" (for this and other abbreviations, see below on this page) 1954], G. GRONAU ["GBA" 1894 and 1895. "NAV" 1894. "RFK" 1908], G. FRIZZONI ["A" 1902], H. COOK [Giorgione, London 1900, and 1904²], U. MONNERET DE VILLARD [Giorgione da Castelfranco, Bergamo 1904], L. JUSTI [Giorgione, Berlin 1908], L. VENTURI [Giorgione e il giorgionismo, Milan 1913. Pitture italiane in America, Milan 1931, and 1933. Giorgione, Rome 1954. Giorgione, in the "Enciclopedia universale dell'arte—VI" 1958], G. F. HARTLAUB [Giorgione Geheimnis, Munich 1925], R. LONGHI ["VA" 1927. Viatico per cinque secoli di pittura veneziana, Florence 1946], A. VENTURI [Storia dell'arte italiana —IX, 3. Milan 1928], L. HOURTICQ [Le problème de Giorgione, Paris 1930], H. POSSE ["JPK" 1931], J. WILDE ["JKSW" 1932], G. GOMBOSI ["BM" 1935], W. SUIDA ["GBA" 1935. "AV" 1954], D. PHILLIPS [The Leadership of Giorgione, Washington 1937], G. M. RICHTER [Giorgio da Castel-franco, Chicago 1937], G. FIOCCO [Giorgione, Bergamo 1941, and 1948². "RV" 1955], A. MORASSI ["LA" 1939. Giorgione, Milan 1942. "BM" 1951. "AV" 1954], G. DE BATZ [Giorgione and his Circle, Baltimore 1942], R. PALLUCCHINI [La pittura veneziana del Cinquecento, Novara 1944. I capolavori dei musei veneti,

Venice 1946. "AV" 1959–60], H. TIETZE–E.TIETZE-CONRAT [The Drawings of the Venetian Painters, New York 1944. "AB" 1949], V. MARIANI [Giorgione, Rome 1945], H. TIETZE ["GBA" 1945. "AV" 1947], R. LANGTON-DOUGLAS ["AQ" 1950], F. M. GODFREY ["C" 1951], C. GAMBA ["AV" 1954], L. VON BALDASS ["JKSW" 1955. (-G. HEINZ), Giorgione, Vienna-Munich 1964], P. ZAMPETTI [Giorgione e i giorgioneschi, Venice 1955. "AV" 1955], P. DELLA PERGOLA [Giorgione, Milan 1955], L. COLETTI [Tutta la pittura di Giorgione, Milan 1955], T. PIGNATTI [Giorgione, Milan 1955], S. BETTINI ["MAP" 1955–56], M. FLORISOONE ["ACSA"], C. MÜLLER HOFSTEDE [ibid.], M. CALVESI [ibid.], H. A. NOË ["NKJ" 1960], R. SALVINI ["P" 1961], S. BOTTARI ["UEV"], R. WITTKOWER [ibid.], G. TESTORI ["PA" 1963], C. VOLPE [Giorgione, Milan 1963, C. GARAS ["BMH" 1964].

The following in particular should be consulted on problems of an iconographical character: A. FERRIGUTO [Almorò Barbaro, Venice 1922. Il significato della "Tempesta", Padua 1922. Attraverso i misteri di Giorgione, Castelfranco 1933. "ACSA", "AAAV" 1962], C. GILBERT ["AB" 1952], L. VON BALDASS ["JKSW" 1953], P. HENDY ["AV" 1954], F. KLAUNER ["JKSW" 1955], E. BATTISTI ["E" 1957].

# Abbreviations

A: L'arte
AA: Art in America
AAAV: Atti dell'Accademia di agri-
   coltura, Scienze e Lettere di Verona
AB: The Art Bulletin
ACSA: Atti del XVIII Congresso
   Internazionale di Storia dell'Arte—
   1955 (Venice 1956)
AN: Arte Nostra (Treviso)
AQ: Art Quarterly
AV: Arte Veneta
BA: Bollettino d'Arte
BDI: The Bulletin of the Detroit
   Institute of Arts
BM: The Burlington Magazine

BMH: Bulletin du Musée Hongrois des
   Beaux-Arts
BRM: Berliner Museen
C: The Connoisseur
E: Emporium
F: Frankfurter Zeitung
GBA: Gazette des Beaux-Arts
ILN: Illustrated London News
JKSW: Jahrbuch der Kunsthistorisches
   Sammlungen in Wien
JPK: Jahrbuch der preussischen
   Kunstsammlungen
K: Kunstchronik
LA: Le Arti
MAP: Memorie dell'Accademia

   Patavina di Scienze, Lettere e Arti
NA: Nuova Antologia
NAV: Nuovo Archivio Veneto
NKJ: Nederlands Kunsthistorisch
   Jaarboek
P: Pantheon
PA: Paragone
RFK: Repertorium für Kunstwissen-
   schaft
RV: Rivista di Venezia
UEV: Umanesimo Europeo e Umane-
   simo Veneziano (Florence 1963)
VA: Vita Artistica
VI: Le Vie d'Italia

# Outline biography

Seldom has a painter been so renowned as Giorgione. His name became famous at once, while he lived; time only increased his renown and, as taste changed, it did not grow less, although it was not accompanied by any real understanding of the man and his work. On the contrary his personality was wrapped in legend, and little by little the Giorgione myth was created. The artist's biography, particularly in the seventeenth century, became so corrupted by fanciful details and the body of his work so swollen by attributing to him paintings that were not by his hand but the work of imitators such as Pietro della Vecchia, that scholars were confused. There was even doubt as to whether the painter had ever existed. Nineteenth-century studies, particularly those—already mentioned—carried out by Cavalcaselle and Morelli, rehabilitated Giorgione and rescued his reputation from a confusion of ideas about his life and his work.

*c.* **1477** Giorgio or Zorzi, according to Venetian dialect ("Giorgione" as far as is known was used for the first time only forty years after the painter's death by Paolo Pino [1548]) was born at Castelfranco: the information is derived from the first edition of Vasari's *Vite* [1550]: "Giorgio was born in Castelfranco in the district of Treviso in the year MCCCCLXXVII. In time, from his nature and from the greatness of his mind, Giorgio came to be called Giorgione; and although he was born of very humble stock, nevertheless he was gentle and well mannered throughout his life. He was brought up in Venice and took unceasing delight in the joys of love; and the sound of the lute gave him marvellous pleasure, so that in his day he played and sang so divinely that he was often employed for that purpose at various musical assemblies and gatherings of noble persons. He studied drawing and found it greatly to his taste; and in this nature favoured him so highly, that he, having become enamoured of her beauties, would never

represent anything in his works without copying it from life; and so much was he her slave, imitating her continuously, that he acquired the reputation not only of having surpassed Giovanni and Gentile Bellini, but also of being the rival of the masters who were working in Tuscany and who were the creators of the modern manner. Giorgione had seen some works by the hand of Leonardo, with a beautiful gradation of colours, and with extraordinary relief, effected, as has been related, by means of dark shadows; and this manner pleased him so much that he was for ever studying it as long as he lived, and in oil-painting he imitated it greatly. Taking pleasure in the delights of good work, he was ever selecting, for putting into his pictures, the greatest beauty and the greatest variety that he could find. Nature gave him such a sweet disposition that, both in oil-painting and in fresco, he made certain living

forms and other things so soft, so well harmonised, and so well blended in the shadows, that many of the excellent masters of his time were forced to confess that he had been born to infuse spirit into figures and to counterfeit the freshness of living flesh better than any other painter, not only in Venice, but throughout the world."

In the second edition of the *Vite* [1568] the date of his birth was put forward to 1478 "when Giovanni Mozenigo, brother of Doge Piero, was Doge"; an alteration perhaps due to the difference in the Venetian manner of calculating the date [Della Pergola, 1957].

As for the surname of the painter, whether Barbarella or Barbarelli, as was several times asserted (see 1648 and 1724–35), no valid documentary support exists for this, and the most recent art historians are therefore inclined to dismiss it.

**1504** Probably in this year,

after the death of Matteo Costanzo, the chapel of St George was built in the church of Castelfranco, and Giorgione was commissioned to paint the altarpiece (*Catalogue*, n.12).

**1506** 1 June. Date and inscription on the reverse side of *Laura* in Vienna (see *Catalogue*, n.13).

**1507** 14 August. The Council of Ten orders the payment to Giorgione of twenty ducats for a picture (now lost; see n.86) to be placed in the Audience Hall of the Doge's Palace in Venice: "We, the heads of the Illustrious Council of Ten, bid and ordain you, the noble lord Francesco Venerio, appointed Provisor Salis ad Capsam Magnam [bursar to the treasury], to pay on behalf of the office of works of the Chancellery and the seat of the Council of Ten . . . to Master Zorzi da Castelfrancho, painter, for the picture he is executing to be placed in the Audience

Chamber of the most illustrious Council, 20 ducats . . ." (State Archives, Venice).

**1508** On 24 January (1507 according to Venetian dates) there is another order for the payment to Giorgione for the not yet finished work in the Doge's Palace: "We, the heads of the Illustrious Council of Ten, bid and ordain you, the noble Lord Aloysio Sanuto, Provisor Salis ad Capsam Magnam: to give and pay to Master Zorzi da Castelfrancho, painter, for the canvas he is executing for the new Audience Chamber of the Heads of that most illustrious Council, twenty-five ducats, namely 25, from the money allocated for the building of the audience chamber . . ." (State Archives, Venice).

By 23 May the painting for the Doge's Palace was probably finished [Morassi] as appears from the order for payment for the protecting curtain for the said picture:

*(Top row, left) Presumed self-portrait (three times life size) in the drawing with the View of Castelfranco (Catalogue n.19), (bottom left) in the* Three Philosophers *(n.17); (top right), as David, in the painting in Vienna (n.76) and lastly (bottom right) the engraved copy of the painting discussed here (see page 93). (On the right) Detail of a* Self-Portrait *in Brunswick (n.26).*

"We, the heads of the most Illustrious Council of Ten, bid and ordain you, Lord Aloysio Sanuto, Provisor Salis ad Capsam Magnam: to give and pay to Master Zorzi Spavento, for the curtain for the picture done for the new Audience Chamber, the total amount as it appears in his bill, Lire 35, Soldi 18 . . ." (State Archives, Venice).

In August work was carried out at the Fondaco dei Tedeschi (German mart or commercial centre) which had been rebuilt: ". . . the Germans are beginning to bring in and fix planks, and whilst in the interior everything is being completed painting is being carried on outside." [M. Sanudo, *Diarii*, 1496–1533].

On 8 November Giorgione finished the frescoes for the

Head of Giorgione in the woodcut published in the second edition [1568] of G. Vasari's Vite. The likeness was taken from the Brunswick painting (see page 83); the picture has acquired part of its prestige as evidence of Giorgione's appearance from the fact that Vasari was able to draw from it.

Fondaco dei Tedeschi and, dissatisfied with the payment he had received, he instituted a lawsuit to obtain just compensation for his work, as is shown in a document of the time: "Ser Marco Vidal by order of the illustrious Signoria related to their Excellencies Providers of Salt that justice must be done to master Zorzi of Chastelfrancho in his suit for payment for painting the Fondaco dei Tedeschi and was referred to his Excellency Hieronimo and Ser Alvise Sanudo and many others." [Cadorin, *Memorie . . .* , 1842].

On 11 December a commission of three artists, nominated by Giovanni Bellini, decided in favour of payment for the work at the Fondaco dei Tedeschi: "Ser Lazaro Bastian, ser Vettor Scarpaza [Carpaccio] and ser Vethor de

Matio, painters, elected in the presence of the magistrates Signori M. Caroso da Ca da Pesaro, Zuan Zentani, Marin Gritti and Aloixe Sanudo, Providers of Salt, as appointed deputies to decide on the value of the painting done on the front façade of the Fondaco dei Tedeschi and executed by Master Zorzi da Castelfrancho, having reached agreement, declared that in their judgment and opinion the said Master Zorzi merited for the said painting the sum of 150 ducats. On the said day, with the agreement of the aforementioned Master Zorzi, 130 ducats were paid to him." [Cadorin, *Memorie . . .* , 1842].

**1510** From the letter of 25 October, quoted below, in which Isabella d'Este,

Marchioness of Mantua, asks Taddeo Albano for a "Night" (that is a *Nativity*) by Giorgione, he having died, perhaps from the plague which raged in Venice in September of that year [M. Sanudo, *Diarii*].

"Most noble Friend: We understand that amongst the goods and estate of the painter Zorzo da Castelfrancho there is a picture of a Nativity, very fine and unusual; if this be so, we would like to have it; therefore we pray you to go with Lorenzo da Pavia and some other person of judgment and reliability, and see if it be an excellent thing; and if you find it to be so, make use of the good offices of our distinguished compatriot Carlo Valerio and whoever else seems good to you to reserve this picture for us, finding out the price and informing us of it.

And should it seem to you necessary to conclude the transaction, in the event of the work being a good one, for that it may be acquired by others, do what you think fit; we are assured that you will act loyally and entirely in our interest, and on sound advice . . . Mantua XXV oct. MDX" [A. Luzio, *Archivio Storico dell' Arte*, 1888].

On 7 November Taddeo Albano replied to Isabella of Mantua, confirming that Giorgione had died as the result of the plague, and he declared that he regretted he could not satisfy her desire because there were no paintings by Giorgione for sale:

"Most illustrious and excellent lady, I have done as your Excellency asked in your letter of the 25 of last month, informing me that you have heard that there was among the effects of Zorzo da Castelfrancho a very fine and unusual picture of a Nativity, and that this being so you would like to have it. To which I reply to your Excellency that the said Giorgione died of plague recently; and wishing to serve your Excellency, I have spoken with some friends who were in close touch with him, and they assure me that there was not such a picture among his effects. It is indeed true that Zorzo painted one for Thadeo Contarini, which from the information I have received is not as good as you would wish. Another painting of the Nativity was done by the said Zorzo for a certain Victorio Becharo, which from what I hear is of better design and superior to the Contarini picture. But the said Becharo is not present in these parts; and, from what I have been told me, neither one nor the other is for sale at any price, since the owners had them for their own enjoyment; so that I regret I have been unable to carry out your Excellency's wishes . . .

"Venice VII november 1510" [A. Luzio, *Archivio Storico dell' Arte*, 1888].

**1525–43** Marcantonio Michiel (the "Anonymo Morelliano") lists many works by Giorgione in the possession of Venetian families (see n.14, 16, 18, 26, 29, 49 and 88–98 in the *Catalogue*).

**1548** Paolo Pino [*Dialogo di Pittura*] mentions a painting by Giorgione, now lost (see n.99).

**1550** From Vasari's *Vite* one finds further references to works by Giorgione (see n.27 and 100 in the *Catalogue*).

**1557** More information is given by Dolce, [*Dialogo . . .* , 1557]: ". . . Giorgio da Castelfranco was commissioned (but a long time ago) to paint the outer façade of the Fondaco dei Tedeschi: and Titian himself, who was young at the time, was commissioned

to paint that part which looked on to the Merceria . . ." (see *Catalogue*, n.22).

**1563** Paris Bordone makes a valuation of the pictures in Giovanni Grimani di Antonio's house, among which is a *Nativity*, now lost (see *Catalogue*, n.101).

**1567** 10 September. In the *Camerino delle Antigaglie* of Gabriele Vendramin there appears to have been a small painting by Giorgione (see n.102).

**1568** In the second edition of the *Vite* Vasari mentions other paintings by Giorgione (see n.22, 26, 27, 80, 103 and 104 in the *Catalogue*).

**1569** 14 March. In the

In the drawing of the View of Castelfranco (Catalogue, n.19) the surrounding city walls of Giorgione's birthplace are recognisable when compared with what remains of them today.

Palazzo Valier, the house presumed to be Giorgione's in Venice in Campo S. Silvestro (it is the building with the little balcony in the centre of the façade facing the campanile) from a nineteenth-century engraving. (On the right) A monument to Giorgione by A. Benvenuti (1878) erected on a small island in the moat round the outer walls of Castelfranco Veneto.

*Camerino delle Antigaglie* mentioned above other works by Giorgione are listed (see n.38 and 39).

**1575** A note on Michiel's manuscript mentions a portrait painted by Giorgione which is now lost (n.98).

**1648** Ridolfi [*Maraviglie . . .* ] — who prints numerous but not always reliable references to Giorgione's works (see n.12, 21, 22, 26, 65, 79, 80, 91, 100, 103, 106–108, 111–114, 116, 117, 119–125, 127, 129–138) tries to gather all the information about the painter's family, or rather the families that boast of having given him birth: "Castel Franco in the district of Treviso and Vedelago Villaggio disputed for a long time as to where Giorgione was born, as did the cities of

Greece over Homer. The Barbarella family of Castel Franco boasts of having given him birth and with reason because he brought them the most sublime honours . . . Some say, however, that Giorgione was born in Vedelago, that his family was one of the most prosperous there and that his father was rich . . ." One notices the contradiction between this "rich father" and Vasari's "born of very humble stock". The "myth" of Giorgione has begun.

**1724–35** Nadal Melchiori [Chronicle of Castelfranco, ms. in the Correr Museum of Venice, cod. Gradenigo Dolfin n.205, page 30] gives the following details concerning the legend created round Giorgione: "Barbarella — This Noble Family lays claim to ancient origins in the city of Milan from where it moved soon after 1400 to Castel Franco . . . To this family Giorgio Barbarella was born, the very celebrated painter . . . In the first chapel called S. Giorgio there is the picture of Our Lady with the child Jesus in her arms and in the bottom right hand corner St George and in that of the left St Francis. This was created by the marvellous and never sufficiently praised brush of Giorgio Barbarella, citizen of Castel Franco, the inventor of tenderness in painting; commonly known as Giorgione because of his great skill, noble behaviour and nature. Tuzio Constanzo commissioned the said Giorgione to paint this picture . . .".

# Catalogue of works

Giorgione is neither a myth, nor a legendary being. He was an historical figure who lived at the end of the fifteenth century and during the first decade of the sixteenth. He played a part and, indeed, a leading one in that particular moment of history – the revival of civilisation in Venice in the humanist and Renaissance sense. He stands in the same relation to Venetian painting as Raphael or Michelangelo to that of Central Italy; that is, he approached the problem of art as a search for inner subjective truth, in full awareness that the individual is a part of a whole to which he is indissolubly linked. Man, nature, the universe: that is the Giorgionesque theme.

Information about him is scarce though fully reliable and very few works can be attributed to him with confidence. But the echoes of his extraordinary personality (Baldassare Castiglione – as has been seen – quotes him [1528] as being one of the five great Italian painters and as unique amongst Venetians) spread quickly, fed by imaginary details and helped by his early death. Seventeenth-century criticism was to create the Giorgione "myth", anxious to bestow a legendary halo on an artist so famous during his short life. The myth grew from the renown that flowered round an innovator on the threshold of the sixteenth century who suddenly outstripped Giovanni Bellini, Carpaccio and Cima da Conegliano in that search for freedom in pictorial expression which remains his greatest glory and which led the way to Titian, Sebastiano del Piombo, Palma Vecchio and many others who could by no means be considered minor artists.

The responsibility for creating the legend must go more to Ridolfi than to Vasari who, though not always an accurate biographer, gives exact and sound criticism of Giorgione's painting ("he began to give his work more softness and greater dimensions by fine painting . . . always pursuing living and natural models . . . insisting that painting in colour alone without any study or drawing was the true way of carrying out his art . . ."). Following Vasari, Ridolfi carried on by giving imaginary information which led to serious misrepresentation, spreading (if he did not invent) the legend that the painter was a member of the Barbarella family. Original sources are silent on the subject. The seventeenth .century added a whole series of vaguely Giorgionesque paintings to the list of Giorgione's authentic pictures.

Many were downright false, carried out in part, as was well known, by Pietro della Vecchia.

In the nineteenth century when scholars wished to make a critical study of the artist, Giorgione's name was almost dropped from the history of art, to such an extent had legend surrounded and confused his personality. The work of revision, undertaken by Cavalcaselle and Morelli, was made easier by the publication [1800] of a book in which Marcantonio Michiel, with the curiosity and taste of the amateur, lists, among other things, all the paintings by Giorgione that he saw in houses in Venice and Padua between 1525 and 1543. The two scholars – one helped by his unusually sound intuition; the other by the comparative method which he had evolved – began their work with documented pictures, and succeeded, if not in reconstructing the painter's personality, at least in giving it a genuine physiognomy and wresting it from myth. In spite of errors and omissions and some inaccurate appraisals and attributions, Cavalcaselle and Morelli laid the foundation for all serious studies on Giorgione. Unfortunately their immediate successors did not profit from it and once more ideas became confused. Cook, accepting as fact discrepancies in the two worthy critics' conclusions, took for granted that all the paintings proposed by both of them were by Giorgione; and Justi subsequently increased their number by adding mediocre works to masterpieces and setting out himself to build up a heterogeneous body of work. Thus the research, so positive in many respects, carried out by the two Italian scholars was rendered useless. Gronau realised this and determined to go again through all the literary evidence and exclude everything not historically verified. Lionello Venturi kept scrupulously to a similar course and his reconstruction of the body of Giorgionesque work [1913] was extremely useful, leading the way to later studies carried out to good purpose by Richter, Wilde, Longhi, Fiocco, Morassi, Suida, von Baldass, Heinz and, amongst others, by Venturi himself.

One of the reasons for the uncertainty about Giorgione is due to the fact that the events in his very short life took shape with extraordinary intensity. To make use of an overworked expression, he was a revolutionary, and to him we owe the emergence of Venetian painting from the placid waters of the fifteenth century in which it had sailed under

the leadership of that great "pilot" Giovanni Bellini: thanks to Giorgione, painting in the first decade of the sixteenth century made more progress than in the thirty or forty preceding years. Giorgione in truth did not remain bound by the technique of Giovanni Bellini, by whom, as well as by Antonello, he was first influenced; he was aware of, and welcomed, the new opinions rising from various other regions; in particular, as Longhi pointed out, from central Italy, that is from Francia and Costa, but not from them alone. The Madonna in the *Adoration* in Washington (certainly by Giorgione and equally certainly a youthful work) must be compared with the type of Madonna painted repeatedly by Perugino, in the Cambio at Perugia, for example, or by Pinturicchio in the Vatican frescoes or in S. Maria del Popolo in Rome: the same pose, the identical movement of the drapery opening like a fan over the Child in his rush basket. What works of this kind were there in Venice? None are known. Vittore Carpaccio certainly was well informed about many aspects of painting in central Italy; and it is not by chance that he is suggested as one of those who perhaps guided Giorgione, either directly or indirectly, in his early work. Carpaccio, in any case, is a more likely source than German engravings, even those by Schongauer that have been mentioned and which are so Gothic in the twisted and writhing folds of their drapery. These engravings are unlikely to have served as models for Giorgione, who was orientated towards classicism rather than tortured rhythms. Contributions from literature and science in which the new culture was steeped must also be taken into consideration. The independence of knowledge, the search for what was true in nature – true in the purest sense, not secondhand truth – the impatience of restraint, questions about the relations between science on the one hand, philosophy and religion on the other, were much in the news at the time and keenly discussed in university circles in Padua, where Pietro Pomponazzi was propounding, not without opposition from the Church, his passionately held theories concerning the natural sciences and the soul. Nor can it be excluded that the young Giorgione was influenced by the neo-Platonism of Padua, calculated to steer him towards a passionate study of nature and man: a study not at all speculative or philosophical but exquisitely lyrical.

Echoes from central Italian painting and certain ideas derived from Paduan philosophy are therefore the two stimuli which have exerted influence over Giorgione's early development. In reality there was only one motive force: the civilisation of humanism beating strongly and with an ever increasing insistence on the doors of Venetian painting, which, until the beginning of the sixteenth century, does not seem to have extended much beyond religious subjects, with, of course, the exception of infrequent essays in portraiture. Even when attempts had been made to go beyond religious themes, they were always confined to allegories of an edifying character or to the exaltation of the glories of Italy. This does not mean that the Giorgionesque vision was exclusively alive to profane subjects and that the painter had not felt the call of sacred themes. Rather, he revealed a hitherto unknown conception of divinity, more human than in the past; and expressed it through personal spiritual experience, merging celestial beings in the universe of all created things, intimately observed and intimately understood. Through love of nature, of its phenomena – the rising and setting sun, fields, trees, mountains, water – his compositions flower without, apparently, any meaning in the sense of illustration.

The first step towards identifying Giorgione's artistic personality is to be made by an examination of the three paintings definitely known to be his: the *Tempest* in Venice, the *Three Philosophers* in Vienna and the Dresden *Venus*. To these can be added – according to ancient tradition – the altarpiece at Castelfranco, *Laura*, now in Vienna, *Christ Carrying the Cross* in the Scuola di S. Rocco in Venice, and what remains of the decoration on the walls of the Fondaco dei Tedeschi (German commercial centre), also in Venice. A number of other paintings, now considered almost certainly by him, are connected with the so-called "Allendale group", that is the series of religious subjects taking their name from the *Adoration of the Shepherds*, formerly part of the Allendale Collection and now in the National Gallery of Art, Washington, with which are associated the *Adoration of the Magi* in London, the *Holy Family* formerly in the Benson Collection and now in Washington and lastly the *Madonna* in Oxford. This group relates to early work, and is preceded by two paintings in the Uffizi which there seems no reason for doubt.

Stylistic research, then, can begin with relative certainty from this solid body of work, especially after the exhibition in Venice in 1955 dedicated to Giorgione, which enabled scholars to make a direct comparison between many canvases. Consequently Giorgione need no longer be looked upon as an impenetrable sphinx, and perhaps the time is not far distant when it will be possible to follow his career with unity of opinion.

As for the characteristics of these early works, modern critics have drawn attention to their almost primitive purity – in the sense in which it is applied to Greek masterpieces – and Roberto Longhi has subtly described them as "pre-Raphaelite". In addition to dwelling on this aspect scholars have thrown light on the importance of the chromatic vision introduced by Giorgione and have pointed out the "tonal" values, that is the synthesis of colour and light, enriched by delicate and very sensitive modulations in the shadows (such as Vasari described in referring to Leonardo), changing, variable, trembling, spreading symphonically over the whole picture, blurring the contours, wearing away the solid shapes which remained essential as long as the principle prevailed that local colour must be put on flat, or even with a three-dimensional purpose, but always within the rigid outlines of the design. In the *Tempest*, therefore, one sees the origins of modern landscape painting. The refinement of this chromatic vision, resulting from gradations of colour and light rather than from a series of intersecting lines, and the relationship between figures and their setting became continually more intimate, while in the fifteenth century the separation between figures and landscape background was still distinct. In spite of the novel liberation of fantasy (which led to important developments in the field of graphic representation) Giorgione succeeded in achieving the supremely dignified monumentality of the *Three Philosophers* in Vienna. From then onwards Venetian artists were to use colour in such a way as to reveal it as a "power of matter to become light" [D'Annunzio].

Nor does Giorgione's brilliant career stop here. In his work he deals with large half-length figures "without drawing", which led Vasari to accuse him of not knowing how to draw. Longhi, in particular, devotes himself to a reconstruction of this technique by studying a number of works, each of which presents extremely interesting problems bristling with implications. These include the relationship between Giorgione and the young Titian and explain why paintings such as the *Sleeping Venus* in Dresden and the *Fête Champêtre* in Paris were attributed first to one and then to the other, or to both, suggesting that Titian worked on Giorgione's pictures after the latter's death. When one bears in mind that for other work, such as the *Adulteress* in Glasgow, Sebastiano del Piombo was given the credit, it will be clear what confusion there was about the output of Giorgione's last years, and one must be on one's guard against the similarities that exist between Giorgione's work and that of the "moderns" – Titian and Sebastiano del Piombo. This, therefore, is the problem: the importance of Giorgione's activity, not only in itself but in regard to the artistic development during most of the sixteenth century. Every painter – including Giovanni Bellini who was already old at the time and who is remembered as one of the possible masters of the young painter from Castelfranco – who became aware of Giorgione's discoveries will have adapted his innovations to his own temperament; however between 1505 and 1515, and to a lesser degree afterwards, the number of paintings revealing the "psychological moment" increased (see below). This was the most striking aspect of Giorgione's later work, and its aura, more or less justly defined as "mysterious", very much intrigued his contemporaries and posterity. Even the inflation of the number of his paintings is a proof of Giorgione's success; and sixteenth-century Venetian historians were so well aware of it that, in their fear of harming the new star Titian – undisputed master of art in the realm of the Venetian Republic and most sagacious manager of his own reputation – they tried to prove that Giorgione's fame was the result of boosting, supposed to have been created

by Titian's adversaries. One has only to read the following passage by Dolce: ". . . Titian . . . solely from that small spark which he discovered in Giorgione's painting, saw and understood how to paint to perfection". Thus, apart from seventeenth-century exaggerations already mentioned, there were difficulties created by modern attempts at clarification, while even in the field of literary criticism, Baroque interpretations – likewise advanced in the seventeenth century and accepted later – added to the already serious confusion and led to the tenacious survival of the "myth".

Since then, however, the situation has been clarified to some extent, and further progress is still possible. If, as everything leads one to believe, *Christ Carrying the Cross* in the Scuola di S. Rocco at Venice is really by Giorgione, then even his activity during his last years will not remain obscure, especially if scholars succeed in proving that the *Fête Champêtre* in the Louvre is by Titian alone. We know that the *Tempest* illustrates no particular incident or, if it does, the subject has no special significance but is merged in a comprehensive vision of life in its most profound and recurring aspects: there is no story, but sheer enchantment; almost the annihilation of the individual in the immensity of creation: a spiritual state of mind similar to that which Giacomo Leopardi defines in his *Infinity*. Giorgione did not aim at dramatic urgency in his figures, as Titian so often did; the human burden, the "psychological moment" is purified and becomes exquisitely subjective contemplation: reality transformed into ecstasy. Because of these cosmic characteristics Giorgione's art transcends his time and appears to us so prodigiously alive and contemporary.

According to the practice in this series of books, the *Catalogue* which follows gives a list of pictures by Giorgione as well as of works attributed to him, though there may be

considerable difference of opinion on the subject. As there is such a heterogeneous body of works – I have tried to show how artists influenced by his innovations were confused with him – it is clear that if it were treated as a single sequence one would create not one "Giorgione", whether new or old, but several Giorgiones, beginning with the Giorgione who emerges from the shadow of Giovanni Bellini and to whom pictures may be attributed which would otherwise be called Bellini; continuing with Giorgione the innovator, and ascribing to him works which in our opinion it would be more reasonable to attribute to Titian, Sebastiano del Piombo or to one of the other innumerable Giorgionesque painters; and ending with a Giorgione who, owing to serious errors – or downright generous acceptance of the claims of the art trade – would be laden with works so inferior as to be wearisome to enumerate. Such a bulky compilation would merely deter the reader from reaching conclusions which, if not absolutely unchallenged, are at least consistent with Giorgione's output. Our list is therefore divided into two parts, the first contains authentic works (that is, their authenticity is supported by written evidence or is almost unanimously accepted) and works which in our opinion (for the most part backed by excellent judgment) show a stylistic similarity such as to suggest a plausible develop-

4

ment, and including works which, although of the highest standard, are not unanimously attributed to Giorgione. In the second list are works which, although thought to be Giorgione's even by authoritative critics, we do not feel able to attribute to him. A third list comprises works mentioned in contemporary, or near contemporary, sources but now lost. A final one enumerates drawings in which, as with paintings in the second list, we do not discern Giorgione's hand.

A brief explanation follows about the technique which, the reader will see, is usually omitted from the list of symbols placed at the head of each description. In point of fact the exact medium used by Giorgione has not yet been explored in detail, nor can it always be assumed that he painted in oils. As he worked after Antonello's visit to Venice – old historians say that the latter was the first to use such oil colours – Giorgione probably used a "mixed" technique, which it is believed was brought from Messina to Venice: a technique based on the same pigments formerly used for tempera, but treated with new essences put on in successive coats, and where ingredients typical of the oil procedure were more and more used until – perhaps – the method could be described as genuine painting in oils. But the works which seem to show the use of this painting in oils are among the number which reveal the hand of artists who followed Giorgione or which can definitely be attributed to Titian or others.

Finally: the question of date: readers will find many gaps. To establish an exact chronology for an artist such as Giorgione, whose known work was completed within ten years and may even have taken no more than five, and which contains virtually no certain fixed point in time, presents a desperately difficult undertaking: all the more so, one must add, in that various paintings give the impression, even in certain cases, such as the *Tempest*, of having been left for a long time in his studio, and subjected sometimes to considerable elaboration, dictated by second thoughts (not difficult to imagine in a

man of Giorgione's temperament, a reflective artist continually spurred on by the desire for novelty). Thus we have preferred to limit ourselves to an order which, in our opinion, conforms with the development of the master and which must have taken place – as regards fully authentic works – between the first years of the sixteenth century and 1510, with an "introductory period" (including, approximately, everything earlier than the Pellizzari frescoes) covering the last years of the fifteenth century. To attempt greater precision would not be honest from the point of view of criticism.

**1** ⊞ ⊗ 89 × 72 ▤∶
*1505
**The Trial of Moses by Fire**
Florence, Uffizi
This illustrates an episode in the life of Moses from the rhymed Bibles of Herman de Valenciennes and Geofroy de Paris: the future patriarch, when still a baby, is subjected to the trial by fire so that he may explain why in jest he had let fall Pharaoh's crown from his head. In the presence of the sovereign on the throne the child, taking a burning coal from the brazier, puts it in his mouth, burns his tongue and remains a stammerer for life. The scene, set against a panoramic background, conveys an atmosphere of contemplation, almost of enchantment, very different, for example, from Poussin's picture of a similar subject now in the Louvre. In 1692 the painting was listed, together with the next one (n.2), among the art treasures of the Grand Duchess of Tuscany at Poggio Imperiale; in 1795 it went to the Uffizi as a Giovanni Bellini, which was a shrewd judgment for those days. Cavalcaselle [1871] thought that both paintings were by Giorgione. Fiocco [1941], pointing out how frequently he left his paintings unfinished, suggested that he might have worked in collaboration with Giulio Campagnola. Morassi agreed but identified the assistant as Catena. L. Venturi, too, thought it was a work of collaboration, and correcting his earlier opinion of 1913 stated [1954]: "The skilful delineation and the splendid colour indicate that Giorgione was responsible for the group of figures on the left, while those on the right, which show a falling off in quality, were certainly painted by another hand." According to Longhi [1946] many of the figures are by "an unknown Ferrarese collaborator, such as Ercole or Mazzolino". It is widely accepted that Giorgione thought out and elaborated the general composition, but that he himself executed only a part of the painting. The attribution of part of the picture to Catena is particularly interesting because he and

1 (Plates I–II)                    2

Giorgione must have been in close touch, as is shown by the inscription on the back of the *Laura* in Vienna (n.13); in any case the picture's extraordinary beauty and unity of conception cannot be denied. The stylistic differences noticed between the various figures may be caused by restoration and not the work of collaborators. This is one of Giorgione's early works: the female figure, full face, looking out from the picture seems to be a forerunner of the *Judith* in Leningrad (n.5); and the other figures are Giorgione's ideal types, in fact an

5 (Plate XX)

*Copy of an engraving by Antoinette (Toinette) Larcher (c. 1690) of the painting n.5 before it was cut down.*

assembly of his best-known characters. Finally the landscape, so vivid, so flooded with light, with breezes blowing between trees and rocks, shows for the first time that love of nature which was to become typical of Giorgione's poetic approach.

## 2 ⊞ ✦ 89×72 *1505* 🔲 ⦂
### The Judgment of Solomon
Florence, Uffizi

The same "external" characteristics and the same formal composition as in the preceding picture and, as it illustrates a biblical episode (*Kings*, 1), also similar in theme. Solomon is seated on a throne (as is Pharaoh in the other painting); at his feet stands a group of

dignitaries and the two women who await judgment, while a man in armour holds in his left hand the living child; the dead child, not acknowledged by either woman, is lying on the ground. As the "external" events can be compared with those in the picture of Moses, Cavalcaselle attributes it also to Giorgione, but it has also been criticised on the grounds that it reveals very considerable help from assistants. Berenson [1936] attributes only the landscape to Giorgione; Richter [1937] avoids expressing a personal view and quotes F. Harck [1896] who pronounced it definitely a copy; Fiocco [1941] thinks that the idea for the composition may just possibly have been Giorgione's but that Giulio Campagnola carried it out ("In the *Trial by Fire* the figures glow, while in the *Judgment* it is the landscape that reveals Giorgione's hand and inspiration"); Morassi, too, points out that in the *Judgment* the figures are inferior to the landscape background which is perhaps even finer than in the *Trial by Fire*; L. Venturi [1954] concurs in this opinion. In reality, this painting — and its pendant — is very important in reconstructing the artist's youthful activities. If compared with the Washington *Adoration* (n.8) and the others in the Allendale group (n.6, 7, 11), it exceeds them in brilliance. Figures and landscape are decisive elements; here for the first time are the typical rocks, curious, delicate, almost soft, like pure wax full of pale honey, still a little rigid, but already vaguely anthropomorphised as will be seen in other pictures from the *Three Philosophers* (n.17) and the *Tramonto* (n.18) to the *Tempest* (n.16), characteristics so easily identifiable, so unusual and personal as to leave no doubt about Giorgione's hand whenever one comes across them. Here, too, are the luminous small pebbles, like minute pearls, vibrating with light, which appear in several of his pictures. Finally, the pastoral incident in the centre of the composition accords perfectly with that in the above-mentioned *Adoration*, where the two figures are painted with the same rapid, nervous brush strokes as in the *Judgment*. The enormous oak tree dominating the scene belongs to the same family as the trees in the Leningrad *Judith* and even in the *Tempest*. The rendering of the human beings is quite new, that is Giorgionesque: they are painted with colour laid over colour, in the same way as in the Benson *Madonna* (n. 6), the Oxford *Madonna* and in other youthful works.

## 3 ⊞ ✦ ——— 🔲 ⦂
### Various Instruments, Medallions and Scrolls
Castelfranco Veneto, Casa Pellizzari, called "Giorgione's House"

This is a frieze in monochrome of fine yellow ground, with touches of white for the highlights and sepia-coloured shadows, on the upper surface of the longer walls (north-east and south-west) of a large hall, formerly divided into two rooms, in the Pellizzari house (first belonging to the Marta family and now to the Tourist Information Bureau) near the Duomo. Traditionally it is the home of the Barbarella family of which, according to some versions, Giorgione was an illegitimate offspring. The painted band is about 76.5 cm. high and runs for about 1,585 cm. along each wall, but there are large gaps, recently restored merely in order to give an idea of the continuity of the lost composition. It is probable that the frieze originally ran along the shorter walls: in fact at each corner of the south-east wall there is a fragment of fresco (about 90 cm. long) which matches the rest of the decoration; there may also have been frescoes on the longer walls on the coping of old doors and windows now blocked up. The instruments portrayed, gathered together in most cases to form trophies, probably illustrate the various liberal and mechanical arts; the medallions simulate large cameos; mottoes in Latin are written on the scrolls. Pignatti [1955] compares the allegorical figures illustrating the liberal arts with the *Sphaera Mundi* of Sacrobosco, published in Venice in 1484 or 1485. Lorenzi removed some fragments from the fresco at the end of the nineteenth century; other areas emerged in the course of restorations carried out in 1955. This discovery and the cleaning of parts already known have confirmed the importance of the cycle, to whose Giorgionesque character Cavalcaselle had already drawn attention. Borenius and Richter were also inclined to recognise Giorgione's hand. Morassi thinks that a collaboration between painter and pupils is more likely; whereas Fiocco [1948] believes it to be quite definitely Giorgione's earliest work. Although it is impossible to give a reliable opinion about frescoes in such a damaged condition and with so much missing, it seems reasonable to attribute them to Giorgione; certain stylistic elements are reminiscent of his youthful work, in particular of his two pictures in the Uffizi: for example the rapid brush work noticeable in some of the little figures in the fresco is apparent in the chiaroscuro painting on Pharaoh's throne, in n.2; while the mathematical and geometrical symbols can be compared with those in the painting in Vienna (n.17).

A medallion with the profile of a Roman emperor in Casa Rostirolla, also in Castelfranco, is associated with the Pellizzari cycle, among the number of fragments removed by Lorenzi.

*(Above) View of part of the Casa Pellizzari at Castelfranco Veneto, with the frieze described in n.3; in the background the north-west wall; on the sides, the walls with the surviving decoration (which perhaps ran round the other two sides). Detail of the south-east wall, with fragments of fresco, probably connected with the frieze in existence at the top of the longer walls.*
*(Below) Detail of the south-west wall, with remains of the paintings (definitely not connected with the above fresco) above a blocked-up opening. Other traces of similar frescoes remain above blocked-up doors and windows in the building.*

## 4 ⊞ ✦ 51×81 🔲 ⦂
### Sacra Conversazione
Venice, Accademia

For a long time it was neglected by critics and vaguely attributed to Giorgione's school [Cavalcaselle, 1, 1912]: Previtali, Catena and others were suggested as possible authors. Gronau connected it with the Allendale *Nativity* and the Benson *Holy Family*, attributing them all to an unknown follower of Giorgione, but later [1938] to Giorgione when he was very young. Already by 1927 Longhi had put forward the hypothesis that the painting was certainly by Giorgione. Suida [1935] tended to agree with him, as did Morassi. Pallucchini [1944], on the other hand, suggested Sebastiano del Piombo, pointing out

affinities with his known work. According to this scholar the artist shows "a formal and constructive interpretation of Giorgionesque colour orchestrated with light tones so that the texture of the planes is made very clear"; moreover "the scene, considered as a whole, has a severe rectangular form, a firm, solid, architectural weight, very different from the effect that Giorgione was gradually achieving in compositions of this period such as *The Tempest*. The painting, in fact, is very close to the Oxford *Madonna* (n.11); the Virgin's face is painted with the same recourse to pink flesh-colour in depicting the features as indeed in the small figures in the two Uffizi paintings (n.1 and 2).

(Above) The frieze on the
north-east wall.
(Below) The frieze on the
opposite wall. Grey patches
indicate missing parts.

**5**  144×66,5

**Judith**
Leningrad, Hermitage
The biblical heroine carries a
sword in her right hand and is
putting her left foot on the
decapitated head of Holo-
fernes. The work was taken by
Forest from Italy to France at
the end of the seventeenth
century; it was then in the
Bertin Collection, was acquired
by Pierre Crozat (1729), and
passed (by inheritance) to
Louis-François Crozat; after
the latter's death (1772) it
went, with the rest of his
collection, to Catherine of
Russia. During most of the
nineteenth century it was
attributed to Raphael; in 1864
Waagen suggested that it was
by Moretto da Brescia; then
Penther had an intuition that it
might be by Giorgione and
mentioned this idea to Morelli
[1891] who was doubtful.
Gradually, however, critics
have come to accept this
opinion and today its author-

ship is no longer in doubt.
Originally on wood, the
painting was transferred to
canvas in 1838; at this time
it was cut down by 13 cm. on
both sides. It is well preserved
except for a small amount of
restoration: particularly that
on the face, which covers up a
crack in the original wood.

**6**  45,5×36,5
                    *1505*

**Holy Family
(Benson Madonna)**
Washington, National Gallery
of Art (Kress Bequest)
This is probably the picture
sold by Allard van Everdingen
in 1709; in 1887 it was
acquired by Henry Willett of
Brighton; it then passed into
the Benson Collection from
which it took its name. Cook
[1900], and later Justi, put
forward the suggestion that it
was by Giorgione. Phillips
[1909] proposed a close
comparison with the *Nativity*,
later known as the Allendale
*Nativity* (n.8). L. Venturi
[1913] welcomed the idea
that the two paintings were
by the same hand, but named
Catena as the painter of them
both; nevertheless later [1954]
he accepted Cook's suggestion,

as have Suida, Richter,
Morassi, Pignatti and others.
Without doubt it is a youthful
work of Giorgione, going back
to the very beginning of the
century. As well as showing
the influence of Bellini one
notices the fullness of the
drapery exaggerated by the
play of folds reminiscent of
Gothic practice. Morassi
explained this as being derived
from German engravings, in
particular those by Schongauer
and Dürer. The painting is in
good condition. There are a
few light horizontal scratches
round the Madonna's face and
in other areas in the centre.

**7**  29×81

**The Adoration of the Magi**
London, National Gallery
The traditional figures are
shown in front of a barn
between the pillars of a ruined
building. In 1882 this painting,
attributed to Giovanni Bellini,
belonged to the Miles
Collection at Leigh Court.
In 1884 it was acquired by the
National Gallery, but Morelli
had already [1880] changed
the attribution to Catena: an
opinion shared at first by
L. Venturi and Berenson. Only

later did Berenson and
Venturi, and not without some
doubt, accept Cavalcaselle's
view that the artist was
Giorgione. Phillips on the other
hand [1909] thought it was
the work of the "Master of
the Beaumont *Adoration*" (see
n.8). Richter [1937] went back
to Giorgione but insisted that it
was an early work carried out
when the artist was working
under Giovanni Bellini.
Morassi finally accepted
Cavalcaselle's opinion that it
was painted by Giorgione,
and Gould and others agreed,
although Pignatti [1955]
remains uncertain. Stylistically
it has affinities with the so-
called Allendale group (see n.8)
and it accords perfectly with
Giorgione's early work when
he was still influenced by
Bellini and Carpaccio. It was
restored in 1947.

**8**  89×111,5

**The Adoration of the
Shepherds
(Beaumont Adoration;
Allendale Nativity)**
Washington, National Gallery
of Art (Kress Bequest).
The figures are placed in front
of a natural grotto in a land-

scape clearly typical of the
Veneto, immersed in evening
light; on the left in the
background sits a little figure
in the entrance to a small barn.
Present day critics tend to
think this picture may be the
"Night" in Beccaro's house,
mentioned in the letter from
T. Albano to Isabella Gonzaga
(see *Outline Biography*, 1510);
it could, with less certainty, be
the picture belonging in 1563
to Giovanni Grimani, valued
by Paris Bordone at "ten
ducats" (ibid.) which was
later included in the collection
of King James II of England.
At the beginning of the last

Drawing at Windsor Castle
sometimes connected with the
painting n.8, but usually
considered a copy which was
not made by Giorgione.

century it was certainly in
Rome, in the possession of
Cardinal Fesch who sold it
(1845) as a work by Giorgione.
It then passed to the Beaumont
Collection in London and from
there to Viscount Allendale
(hence its above-mentioned
name); finally it was bought
by Duveen who sold it to
S.H. Kress, who bequeathed
it to the National Gallery of
Art in Washington. From early
times it was attributed to
Giorgione, and Cavalcaselle
accepted this, as did Berenson
later (he postulated Titian's
hand in the landscape)
although at first he thought it
was by Catena. Most recent
scholars – from Gronau to
Longhi, Morassi, etc. – agree
that Giorgione painted it, and
on this assumption they also
ascribed to him other paintings
already assembled by Phillips
["BM" 1909] under the
conventional name of "Master
of the Beaumont *Adoration*",
known also as the "Allendale
group" (see n.6, 7, 11). As
already mentioned, the present
composition has been thought
to derive iconographically
from prints by Schongauer.
But it is more likely that
Giorgione had before him
similar subjects by Perugino

**6** (Plate VII)

**7** (Plates VIII–XII)

**8** (Plates XIII–XVI)

**9**

and Pinturicchio, as one notices similarities in style. The paintings in the Allendale group are remarkable for the purity of their composition and the softness of the treatment of colour, used to obtain unusual atmospheric values and luminous effects which do away with the necessity for linear definition.

## 9 ▦ ⊗ 91×115 ▤ ⋮
**The Adoration of the Shepherds**
Vienna, Kunsthistorisches Museum
The painting reached Vienna

10

11 (Plates XVII–XIX)

12 (Plates XXI–XXIX)

from the collection of the Archduke Leopold William. In an inventory of 1659 it is listed as Giorgione; but this has had little following (Fiocco, Coletti and others attribute it to the school of Giorgione; Baldass and Heinz [1964] assign it to Titian); probably influenced by its bad condition. Of the two "Nights" mentioned by T. Albano in his letter to Isabella Gonzaga (see *Outline Biography* 1510) this painting can perhaps be identified [Morassi] with that "not very perfect" one in Contarini's

## 10 ▦ ⊗ 44×36,5 ▤ ⋮
**Madonna and Child**
Leningrad, Hermitage
At first attributed to the school of Giovanni Bellini; then Justi [1908], Fiocco, Morassi and others ascribed it to Giorgione; Berenson was silent on the subject (or thought it the work of a follower [1954]) and Coletti and others rejected the idea of Giorgione. In the Venice exhibition of 1955 it was shown as an authentic novelty, very few scholars having seen it before. We agree with Morassi in thinking it an early Giorgione, one of the freshest; painted, it seems with Raphael in mind. The landscape, on the other hand, is typical of Giorgione: rocks, hills, gentle and broken up, the little tower, all bathed in noonday sunlight: anticipating his greater achievements in the density of the background with mutually related colours. Originally on wood; transferred to canvas in 1872 and perhaps fairly extensively repainted at that time (Fiocco speaks of "Giorgione and restorers") but not so seriously as to conceal the master's hand.

## 11 ▦ ⊗ 76×60 ▤ ⋮
**Madonna Reading**
Oxford, Ashmolean Museum
Through the window one sees the Riva degli Schiavoni with the Doge's Palace and the S. Marco campanile still without its sixteenth-century pyramidal apex. The picture can be identified with the Duke of Tallard's painting, attributed to Giorgione and sold in Paris in 1756 ("The Virgin seated and reading, the

house. It seems clear that there is no question of this one having been copied by another hand; it is a replica by the master. This is shown by elements in the design and by the colours which have emerged during a recent [1955] restoration. In the landscape there are considerable differences between the two pictures. In the Washington painting there is a large tree with a great circular sweep of leafy foliage; in this one the tree is reduced to a slender sapling with few leaves. Above all the light is quite different: almost daylight in the Allendale *Nativity*, but here evening light, with typical sunset colours in a sky blurred by mists, with shadows in the foreground.

Child Jesus lies in front of her. In the background, the Place of St Mark in Venice") and also with the painting which belonged in the nineteenth century to the Earls of Cathcart, whose descendants put it up for sale in London in 1949 as a Cariani. It was bought by the Ashmolean and was immediately claimed as a Giorgione [Parker, 1949]. The direct connection with Giorgione was upheld by Pallucchini [1949], Gronau [1949], Morassi [1951], L. Venturi [1954] and by almost all scholars today, except Berenson who favoured a follower. It is in fact a notable discovery, throwing light on the painter's early life: "There is no doubt that on stylistic grounds the Oxford *Madonna* fits easily into the group of paintings – the *Adoration of the Magi*, the Benson-Duveen *Holy Family*, the so-called Allendale *Adoration of the Shepherds* – ...; a group of works which prepares the way for ... the *Madonna and Saints* in the Cathedral at Castelfranco" [Pallucchini]. The

The Warrior Saint *(London, National Gallery)* perhaps a copy by a student of the figure in n.12.

treatment of the landscape background is so summary as to appear unfinished; perhaps the artist wished to express in this way the atmospheric vibrations, made all the more clear by contrast with the foreground.

## 12 ▦ ⊗ 200×152 ▤ ⋮
**Enthroned Madonna and Child, between St Liberale and St Francis (Castelfranco Altarpiece)**
Castelfranco Veneto,
Church of S. Liberale
The knight in armour has been thought to be St George, but

13 (Plate XXX)

*(On the left) The painting n.13 before restoration in 1932. Detail of the same work, in the picture (after 1659) by D. Teniers the Younger, showing the gallery of the Archduke Leopold William in Brussels (Madrid, Prado).*

it seems unnecessary to question his identity. The armorial bearings on the base of the throne are those of the family of the soldier of fortune Tuzio Costanzo. Ridolfi [1648] was the first to claim that Giorgione painted this picture and this has never been disputed. There is, however, disagreement about the date. Gronau, Richter and others, while accepting that it was commissioned for the Costanzo chapel, maintain that the altarpiece was painted before the death of Matteo, son of Tuzio, in 1504: today it is agreed that Tuzio commissioned the painting to commemorate Matteo's death. L. Venturi [1913] perceived here the successful realisation of a creative synthesis between Giorgione's religious feeling and his love of nature. Longhi [1946] thought that the perspective structure, breaking away from Bellini's examples, tended towards the Umbrian-Emilian practice of Costa. Judged as a whole, the little altarpiece does not depart from Venetian compositions of the time; rather the painter seems to reduce the subject of the *Sacra Conversazione* to its essentials; but in combining the various parts he reveals quite new ideas: in front of the high parapet he creates an interior dominated by the Virgin's high throne; whilst the raised viewpoint allows us to see not only the screen but the silent country-side with the turreted town on the left and the mountains on the right and two small figures in the middle distance. The saints stand as if cast down on to a lower plane, and alone the Madonna solemnly dominates the foreground scene. It is the figure of the Madonna that unites the two zones, welding them together in perfect unity, helped also by the warm golden light which encompasses human beings and objects in one harmony and throws round them an aura of enchantment. The painting had been restored several times before 1931 when M. Pellicioli took measures to reinforce the whole painted surface.

In the National Gallery in London there is a painting (39 × 27) of the knight. Following Cavalcaselle, some scholars – among them Morassi and Della Pergola (taking it for a St George) – consider it a preliminary sketch, while others – from Fiocco [1941] onwards – think, perhaps more justifiably, that it is student's copy.

**14**

**15**

**13** ▦ ✦ 41×33,5 1506 ▤ ⋮

**Portrait of a Young Woman (Laura)** Vienna, Kunsthistorisches Museum Canvas mounted on panel. According to Richter [1937], this enigmatic figure could be a courtesan, perhaps portrayed as Daphne or as a poetess, in which case the leaves suggest that she had been crowned with laurels, or suggest a hope that she would be. It seems, however, more reasonable to think that this is a painting of a woman whose name was Laura and who also sat, no doubt, for the woman in the *Tempest* (n.16). The picture is mentioned for the first time in 1659 as by an unknown artist when it belonged to the Archduke William Leopold's collection in Brussels. Later it was ascribed to a painter of the Venetian School, then to Romanino [Engerth, 1882] and to Boccaccino [A. Venturi] In the same year Dollmayr [1882] discovered the original inscription on the back: "In 1506 on June 1 this was painted by the hand of master Zorzi da Chastel fr[anco], colleague of master Vincenzo Chaena [that is, Catena] . . ."; but this interesting discovery was not enough to dispel uncertainty. Finally in 1908 Justi attributed it with some doubt to Giorgione, Hourticq [1930] agreed, and Giorgione's authorship was confirmed without reservations by Longhi [1927]. This last opinion has been supported by modern critics, beginning with Wilde [1931]; only Richter remained doubtful because he had not examined the canvas after its restoration. The inscription mentioned above is of the greatest importance; it gives us a work dated by Giorgione – perhaps the only one (but see n.24).

**14** ▦ ✦ 48×42 ▤ ⋮

**Boy with an Arrow** Vienna, Kunsthistorisches Museum In 1531 Michiel made a note that in the collection of Giovanni Ram, in Venice, the "picture of the head of a boy who holds an arrow in his hand was by Zorzi da Castelfranco"; the next year this scholar saw the same painting in the possession of Antonio Pasqualino, and pointed out that the former owner also had a copy of it, thought by him to be an original. In 1663 it passed from the collection of the Archduke Sigismund of Austria to Ambras Castle near Innsbruck and, a century later (1773), to the Imperial Collections in Vienna. Critics do not all agree in identifying the painting in Vienna with that mentioned by Michiel, and it has been attributed to several other painters. The name of Andrea del Sarto was suggested [the Ambras catalogue, 1663] and Schedone [Mechel, Catalogue of the Imperial Collections, 1783]. More recently Berenson [1932 and 1936] ascribed it

to Lotto, as did Buschbeck [1954]; while Boehn [1908] thought it was a Correggio, and Mündler and Waagen suggested Bernardino Gatti. According to L. Venturi [1954], "it is certainly in the Giorgionesque manner but it could be a copy of a lost original". Ludwig, Wickhoff, Fiocco, Morassi, Coletti all

**16** (Plates XXXI–XXXVIII)

think it is by Giorgione himself; Gronau takes it for a copy; Richter and Wilde are uncertain. In our opinion it is an original painting, perhaps remotely influenced by Leonardo.

**15** ▦ ✦ 61×51 ▤ ⋮

**Shepherd with Flute** Hampton Court, Royal Collection According to Richter [1937], the youth is Apollo, but the above title is usually given to it. It was bought by King Charles I of England as a Giorgione. In 1649 it passed to the De Critz Collection, in 1688 to that of King James II, and in 1714 to that of Queen Anne. Most modern critics, beginning with Morelli [1880], agree that it is by Giorgione; but Justi, Richter and Morassi have raised doubts; A. Venturi [1928] thought it might be by Torbido. However, the painting seems to possess much of the subtlety of Giorgione's authentic work: the face, which, by means of light and colour, emerges from the darkness of the background, belongs to his world; it even has something of the vision to be seen in Leonardo's work; as has the *Boy with an Arrow*, with which it has many affinities.

**16** ▦ ✦ 82×73 ▤ ⋮

**The Tempest** Venice, Accademia It is one of the very few paintings that critics have always and unanimously attributed to Giorgione. Opinions differ widely,

however, about its subject and date. In the Vendramin Collection (1569) it is described as "Mercury and Isis". Many writers have since then tried to solve the problem of its meaning: according to Ferriguto, Giorgione has created an allegory of nature, and Richter thinks he has portrayed the infancy of Paris; Morassi believes that Giorgione intended an allusion to himself, that is, to the often-mentioned supposition that he was illegitimate; L. Stefanini [1955] is of the opinion that the theme was taken from the *Hypnerotomachia Poliphili* by Francesco Colonna ("Steeped in the spirit of the *Hypnerotomachia*, every element in the picture dissolves into the next. The eye follows without difficulty the artist's whim, which plays audacious tricks with nature, selecting from it, and refining, in an attempt to realise his inspiration"). Other scholars have recently suggested that the subject is the nymph who suckles Epapho's son under the watchful care of Mercury; or the finding of Moses. The many different explanations, even if interesting, though never entirely convincing, should not deflect attention from the painting's great qualities. They satisfy one's sense of beauty without it being necessary to search for hidden meanings which may after all not exist. The work belongs to the small number listed by Michiel [1530]. He saw it in 1530 in Gabriele Vendramin's house and described it as follows: "The small landscape painting with the storm and with the "cingana" (gypsy) and soldier is by the hand of Zorzi da Castelfranco". In 1569 it was still in the Vendramin Collection; in 1856, it was in the Manfrin Collection. Prince Giovannelli acquired it in 1875 and in 1932 sold it to the

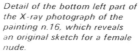

Italian government. Michiel's description, going back to about twenty years after the artist's death when the painting was still owned by the man who had in all likelihood received it from Giorgione himself, is much simplified but perhaps the closest to the spirit of the picture. L. Venturi towards the

*Detail of the bottom left part of the X-ray photograph of the painting n.16, which reveals an original sketch for a female nude.*

end of 1913 justly said: "The subject is nature: man, woman and child are only elements – not the principal features – of nature". Nature here reveals its primordial strength in profound and mysterious phenomena. The stormy sky, rent by a sudden flash of lightning; the pure figure of the woman clasping her child to her breast; the young man standing on the left; and the stream, the ruins, which allude to passing time and fading splendours; the background with the battle-mented walls and trees: all form a unity showing life's perpetual growth and change. This exaltation of natural forces is conveyed in a painting in which light clothes everything in a tremulous golden atmosphere and shares in every figurative detail, whether flesh or sky, architecture or branches stirring gently beneath the weight of the summer squall, where every-thing seems to lose its indivi-dual plastic consistency and become the pure expression of art.

An X-ray examination has revealed that Giorgione first painted another female nude in the foreground where the youth now stands. This discovery seems to show that the artist had no intention of illustrating any particular theme, but was allowing his imagination to guide him,

modifying the composition
until he had found the lyrical
form which best suited him.
As for the date, Cook suggests
before 1500; Conti [1894]
and Borenius date it earlier
than the Castelfranco
altarpiece (n.12); but almost
all other modern scholars
later than it.

**17** 123,5×144,5

**The Three Philosophers**
Vienna, Kunsthistorisches
Museum
The meaning of this picture has
been the subject of much
dispute. In an inventory of
1659 (see below) it was
described as "The Three
Mathematicians"; in that of
Mechel [1783], as "The Three
Magi who are awaiting the
rising of the star". In the
nineteenth and twentieth
centuries interpretations came
thick and fast: Janitschek
[1871] thought that the three
figures symbolised the world
of antiquity, the medieval
world and the modern world;
Wickhoff [1895] identified the
men with Evander, Pallas and
Aeneas; Schaeffer [1910]
suggested Marcus Aurelius
with two philosophers. Others
put forward many different and
even less convincing
interpretations. Ferriguto
[1933], elaborating on
Michiel's already-mentioned
identification of the three men
with three philosophers (see
below) thought they
represented incarnations of

**19** (Plate XLVIII)

**20** (Plate XLVII)

different stages in human
thought: the young man
symbolising the Renaissance;
the man with the turban,
Arabic philosophy; and the
old man with the beard, the
philosophy of the Middle Ages.
Lastly, F. Klauner [1954–55]
in an exhaustive study took up
the thesis regarding the Magi,
developing it to show that the
work was conceived as an
Epiphany; in the grotto on the
left, she says, there must have
been a Holy Family; the three
mysterious men would then
be the three Kings of the
Gospel portrayed as the three
wise men, rather than as
worshippers of the new born
Child: a point of view
deriving from contemporary

Renaissance philosophy,
particularly that of the School
of Padua. It may be mentioned
that the young seated man has
been thought to be a self-
portrait.
The picture is among the
few noted by Michiel: "in
the house of M. Taddeo
Contarini, 1525. The oil
painting of three philosophers
in a landscape, two standing
and one seated, contemplating
the sun's rays, with the rock so
marvellously represented, was
begun by Giorgio da Castelfranco and finished by
Sebastiano Veneziano". In 1659
it was in the Archduke
Leopold William's collection
and the following year Teniers
engraved it in his *Theatrum
Pictorium* as by Giorgione.
It reached its present location
from the Imperial Austrian
Collections. Recently it has
been most efficiently restored
[von Baldass, 1953] with much
improvement to the canvas,
which is now even more
brilliant and alive; for example,
the grotto on the left and the
trees, now so easy to see, had
almost disappeared before
restoration. Whether the
painting has been cut down is
not definitely stated (and
perhaps will never be known). A
copy in oils by David Teniers the
Younger (National Gallery of
Ireland, Dublin) leads one to
assume this, because the
landscape stretches farther in
all four directions, particularly
to the left and right. The copy
in Ireland is a very free
rendering: the seated youth
holds a basin in his hands, as
well as a T-square, and,
quite simply, looks as if he
were drinking soup; the
central figure has been transformed into a peasant who
wears breeches and holds a
stick in his left hand; the third
figure, who has also been
downgraded and become a
peasant, is in breeches, too,
and carries a bundle and
grasps a stick; the whole, one
must confess, at a first glance,
does accord with the
corresponding parts of the
original. (Camesasca suggests
that it could be an intentional
caricature.)
However one may interpret
the meaning, its subject, as
Michiel says, is three
contemplative men. They are
considering nature indepen-

dently, yet united in a common
desire for knowledge. The
sun's rays bring out a rich
variety of colour, giving life to
objects and harmony to
creation, revealing the blue of
the sky, the houses in the
village, the distant mountains,
large trees standing out against
the light and the grotto in
shadow: an atmosphere of
expectation and of awakening
to an enchanting morning.
L. Venturi [1954] writes:
"What gives a halo of poetry
to the picture is that power of
combining pictorial sensitivity
with an understanding of the
romantic conception of the
world which was called
pantheism". The X-ray
photographs published by
Wilde [1932] show that at
first Giorgione had conceived
the figures in a somewhat
different way; the man
standing in the centre was
more definitely oriental, and
the bearded old man had an
aureole round his head. This
is more a matter of curiosity
than anything else, yet it is
interesting, because it shows
how the painter developed his
ideas. As for Sebastiano del
Piombo's collaboration of
which Michiel speaks, it is
difficult to isolate, or to
identify it with certainty,
owing to the superb unity of
the picture. In any case, even
if the painting were finished
by others this cannot have
been during Giorgione's last
years but must date back to an
earlier period after which the
picture would have lain
unfinished for a time.

**18** 73,3×91,5

**Landscape at Sunset
(The Tramonto, Aeneas and
Anchises)** London, National
Gallery
The subject is obscure: a
rocky landscape; beside a lake
in the foreground two people
are resting, one fairly old, the
other young. Modern scholars
think that the former may
perhaps be St Roch in his
capacity as doctor and the
other St Anthony, identifiable
by the pig, seen just above
the water on the extreme right,
(another monster can be
descried in the centre
foreground, emerging from the
water). On a rocky platform
rising from the far side of the
lake St George is fighting the

**17** (Plates XXXIX–XLVI)

*David Teniers the Younger. A very free version of the painting
n.17 (National Gallery of Ireland, Dublin).*

dragon. Among Giorgione's
pictures in Contarini's house
Michiel notes "a large oil
painting of Hades with Aeneas
and Anchises". All trace of this
work was lost until Sangiorgio
[1933] tried to identify it with
the present picture, at that
time in the Donà dalle Rose
Collection in Venice (it then
passed to a private collection
in London and some time
afterward to the National
Gallery); nevertheless it is very
difficult, if not impossible, to
recognise Aeneas and Anchises
in this painting. It must
nevertheless be remembered
that the family of Donà dalle
Rose came into the possession
of a number of paintings in the
Villa Garzoni at Ponte Casale
which formerly belonged to
the Michiel family. As they
had been inherited from that
worthy cataloguer and
collector of Giorgionesque
paintings, nothing, from the
historical point of view,
prevents a work by Giorgione
coming to us through the
Donà dalle Rose family even
if it cannot be identified with
the present painting. Lorenzetti,
who found it abandoned in a
storeroom in the Villa Garzoni,
recognised its importance
and this put him on the right
track. But he did not think the
time was ripe to make a
premature attribution ("Though
Giorgione's inspiration is clearly
recognisable and some areas,
particularly the small central
figures, are of great beauty,
the question of attributing the
picture to him must be

approached with that degree of
caution associated with everything concerning that artist,
in our present state of
knowledge" [1934]).
Lorenzetti's cautious attitude,
also adopted by Richter [1937]
and all the more justified in
the latter because he had not
seen the picture, has since
changed to virtual unanimity
in Giorgione's favour. Longhi
adopted this opinion in 1934
(the title the *Tramonto* is
due to him), also Fiocco
[1941], who some years before
had ascribed it to Campagnola.
Scholars no longer have any
doubts: in fact, the painting is
of great importance, being
similar in style to the *Three
Philosophers* (n.17) as is
shown by the treatment of the
rocks, soft and haunted by

*Engraving by G. Campagnola.
A youth sitting down and the
head of an old man (see n.18).*

**18**

**21 (Plates LII–LVII)**

shadows, and, being obviously of soft limestone, they assume monstrous shapes in harmony with the disquietening atmosphere of the whole conception. Finally the canvas may be compared with an engraving (Albertina, Vienna) which shows a young shepherd (very similar to the so-called Aeneas), beside whom can be seen indistinctly the head of an old man (resembling the supposed Anchises): obvious variations by Campagnola on the theme of Giorgione's *Tramonto*. Arguments arose about the picture's state of preservation; it was said to be ruined by extensive repainting to cover supposed gaps existing when the painting was discovered. A photograph before restoration ["ILN" November 1933] shows, however, that the repainted areas consist only of a few square centimetres.

**19 ⊞ ⊕ 20×29 ▤ :**
**View of Castelfranco and a Shepherd**
Rotterdam, Boymans-van Beuningen Museum
Drawing in red chalk. Until 1707 it was in the Resta Collection; after several journeys it reached its present location. It is almost unanimously accepted as a Giorgione; Justi put forward a few reservations. According to some scholars the young shepherd in the foreground may be a self-portrait painted as a childhood memory.

**20 ⊞ ⊕ 68×59 ▤ :**
**Portrait of an Old Woman**
Venice, Accademia
More uncertainties and suppositions than usual surround this woman who holds the significant motto "in the course of time". The attribution to Torbido – due to the purely accidental resemblance to an old woman in the latter's altarpiece in S. Zeno of Verona, a resemblance confined to the drawing, as, stylistically, the two works are dissimilar – for a long time led critics astray, preventing their realising the high quality of the present picture. Although baffled by the subject, so far removed in its realistic tone from the spirit of Giorgione – or at least from what is thought to be his spirit – one must agree that the pictorial matter is akin in its refined workmanship to the *Tempest* (n.16). Moreover, the subject is full of a profound

understanding of the human predicament: "The artist whilst portraying his human subject with truth has given it, without any traces of objectivity, a transfiguring richness of style . . . the breadth of the pictorial expression annuls any nordic characteristics and prepares the way for a modern classicism which overrides the limits inherent in its realism and poses problems which anticipate those of today". [Moschini, 1949]. G. Fogolari suggested that the old woman might portray the artist's mother, mentioned in the inventory [1569] of the possessions of Gabriele Vendramin. This is all the more likely in that the inventory states that the picture bears the "heraldic arms of the Ca' Vendramin",

*(Above, from the left) Fragment of fresco (Superintendent of Monuments, Venice) from the Fondaco dei Tedeschi doubtfully attributed to Giorgione [Della Pergola]. It would appear from the engraved copy by Zanetti that the youth was a 'Compagno della Calza'.*
*(Below, on the left) Engraved copies, also by Zanetti, of frescoes formerly on the façade of the Fondaco itself, almost certainly painted by Giorgione.*

traces of which can actually be seen on the frame today. Berenson [1954] stressed the affinities in style with the *Tempest* and put forward the idea that Giorgione by this figure had wished to suggest that the "cingana" (gypsy) of n.16 would become "in the course of time" like the old woman in n.20. The attribution proposed by Della Rovere [1903] was confirmed by Monneret de Villard [1904] and taken up again by Berenson himself. Suida, Morassi, Moschini, Palluchini and others approved. L. Venturi is of a contrary opinion.

**21 ⊞ ⊕ 108,5×175 ▤ :**
**The Sleeping Venus**
Dresden, Gemäldegalerie
"The canvas of the naked Venus, sleeping in a landscape, with a small Cupid, was by the hand of Zorzo da Castelfranco, but the landscape and the cupid were finished by Titian"; thus Michiel writes [1525] about a work in the house of Gerolamo Marcello in Venice: and it is generally agreed that he refers to the Dresden picture. It arrived there some time after its purchase (1697) by the dealer Le Roy, on behalf of King Augustus of Saxony. The remark about Cupid, with the added detail that he was holding in his hand a little bird, was repeated by Ridolfi

**22**

[1648]; yet it was not until the restoration of 1843 that the figure of Cupid emerged at the goddess's feet. It is not known when it was painted over; but it appeared to be in such a poor state of preservation that it was again painted out. In 1932 Posse had X-ray photographs made which confirmed the existence of the Cupid. These should have removed all doubt about the identification with the *Venus* mentioned by Michiel, nevertheless modern critics are not unanimous. In the Dresden gallery's first catalogue [1707] Giorgione is given as the artist, in that of 1722 and in all others up to 1846 the painting is ascribed to Titian (in that of 1856 drawn up by Hübner, it is given as a copy of a Titian by Sassoferrato). Morelli re-attributed it to Giorgione and many scholars supported him. But Hourticq [1930] reverted to Titian, backed by Suida and Morassi. Berenson, Della Pergola, L. Venturi, Fiocco, Coletti and others agreed with Morelli. Without doubt Giorgione painted the picture although not the whole of it: probably the nude figure and the rock on the left are his; but the mantle, the Cupid, the landscape on the right, with the hill, the group of houses and the castle (almost exactly the same in Titian's *Noli Me Tangere* in the National Gallery in London) may be by Titian. It is likely that after Giorgione's sudden death the painting was handed over to his young friend and disciple to finish. It was

*Engraving by Zanetti of the Nude of a Young Woman, (see n.22).*

Giorgione's intention to create a contemplative nude in harmony with the surrounding landscape. Titian, with his more dramatic temperament, added a Cupid and the drapery in the foreground which weaken the immediacy of the relationship between the figure of Venus and the setting. Further, the picture is in anything but a good state of preservation as the result of numerous restorations and re-painting. During the 1939–45 war it was stored in a warehouse and suffered no damage. Discovered by the occupying Russian forces and sent to Moscow, for a long time nothing was known about it and it was feared that it was irremediably ruined, but the painting was sent back to Dresden in 1955.

## Decoration of the Fondaco dei Tedeschi

Details have already been given about the payment made for the frescoes carried out by Giorgione in 1508 on the façade of the Fondaco dei Tedeschi (see *Outline Biography*). Vasari mentions

**26** (Plate L)

*(Above) An engraving by W. Hollar ("True portrait of Giorgione . . .", 1650) of the painting n.26 as it probably was in the original.*
*(Below) Detail of the picture by D. Teniers the Younger (Prado, Madrid), related to the above-mentioned work. There is another copy (Budapest) attributed to Palma Vecchio.*

Giorgione's cycle enthusiastically, writing [1550] that there were "heads and parts of figures very well painted, and most vivacious in colouring", then explaining [1568] that the painter "thought of nothing save of creating figures according to his own fancy in order to display his art", so much so — the historian confesses — that "I, for my part, have never understood them, that is to say I have not understood the meaning of the subjects he illustrated; nor have I found anyone who understands them even after all my many enquiries". Ridolfi [1648] is more specific and explains that on the areas of the façade Giorgione designs "trophies, human beings, heads in light and shadow and, in the corners, he draws geometricians who are measuring the globe; perspectives of columns and, among them, men on horseback and other inventions". Zanetti in [*Varie Pitture a Fresco de' Principali Maestri Veneziani*] reproduced some of the figures which were then still visible, although by then they had started to disintegrate and there were missing areas. Together with the fragment described below they constitute the only graphic record of the cycle: neither is enough to give any sort of reliable impression of the original appearance of this vast work.

**22** 🔲 ⊕ 250×140 *1508 📋 ⋮

### Nude of a Young Woman

Venice, Accademia
The fragment and the surrounding plaster was detached in 1937 and restored by M. Pellicioli. In spite of its precarious state it is of extreme importance in investigating Giorgione's mural technique. This was traditional, but skilfully adapted to the particular problem of a site which was both more extensive and more interrupted than was usual in the time of his predecessors.

**23** 🔲 ⊕ 58×46 📋 ⋮

### Portrait of a Young Man (Giustiniani Portrait)

Berlin, Staatliche Museen
The letters "V V" painted in *trompe l'oeil* on the parapet have never been plausibly explained. Probably they are the initials of the man portrayed, who commissioned it or was its first owner. In 1884 the painting passed from the collection of Giustiniani of Padua (hence its title) to J.P. Richter, who attributed it to Giorgione and sold it (1891) to the Berlin museum. Critics have unanimously attributed it to Giorgione, which is most unusual in the case of a picture for which there is no historical documentary evidence whatsoever. According to G.M. Richter [1937] it is an early work ("painted at approximately the same period as the *Judith*") of about 1504; Fiocco [1941] thinks it may have been painted later because it shows the

**27**

**23** (Plate IL)

**25**

**24** (Plate LI)

**28**

characteristics of full maturity ("the first modern portrait in which one does not get the impression of a devout and heroic patron taken straight from an icon, but of the man himself with a slightly melancholy expression"); Morassi places it "only at a slight distance from the *Madonna* of Castelfranco". Undoubtedly it is one of the most fascinating portraits of the early sixteenth century,

with the brush used lightly yet with thick strokes in continual vibration and almost breaking up in contact with the light: a prototype for Venetian painters of the sixteenth century, and also for a wider following.

**24** 🔲 ⊕ 30×26 1508? 📋 ⋮

### Bust of a Man (Terris Portrait)

San Diego (Cal.), Fine Arts Gallery (Putnam Coll.)

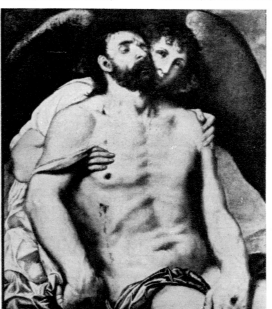

**29**

On the back is an old inscription: "15 . . . by the hand of m. Zorzi da Castelf . . ., which proves, if nothing else, that the work has been attributed to Giorgione for a very long time (some critics have wished to interpret the date as "1508"). In modern times this attribution is supported by Richter, Suida, Morassi, L. Venturi, Coletti and others; while Fiocco [1948] attributes it tentatively to Palma Vecchio. It belonged to the collections of Currov and Terris (hence the name given above).

**25** 🔲 ⊕ 72×56,5 📋 ⋮

### Portrait of a Warrior, in Profile

Vienna, Kunsthistorisches Museum
In 1525 Michiel saw "in M. Hieronimo Marcello's house at S. Tomado: the portrait of this M. Hieronimo in armour, which shows him from the back, at half length, and turning his head, by the hand of Zorzo da Castelfranco". Suida [1954] is in favour of identifying this portrait with the one under discussion, acquired from the Archduke Leopold William and entered in the inventory in 1659 as by Giorgione. In spite of the attribution made so long ago recent criticism has somewhat neglected the painting and even Richter is silent about it. It is true that its condition makes it difficult to judge, but there is no doubt that it is a work of great subtlety. The warrior's profile resembles that of the seated young man in the *Three Philosophers* (n.17); moreover in the *Adoration* in London (n.7) there is a similar example of earlier date in which a warrior in profile (facing the other way) is included. Even the use of colour bears Giorgione's stamp, particularly recalling the treatment in his *Christ Bearing the Cross* at the Scuola di S. Rocco in Venice (n.27) and perhaps that in the central figure in the Detroit picture

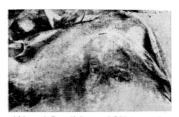

*(Above) Detail (turned 90° towards the right) of the X-ray photograph of n.29 of the area of Christ's ribs, revealing the face of a youth underneath the painting visible today.*
*(Below) A Pietà attributed to various artists (Savings Bank, Treviso), formerly associated with n.29.*

(n.30). In short, in all probability we have here a painting by Giorgione carried out in his later period.

## 26 ⊞⊕ 52×43 ▤⫶
### Self-Portrait
Brunswick, Herzog Anton-Ulrich-Museum
Vasari writes [1568] that in the patriarch Grimani's house there were some most beautiful "heads" by Giorgione, in particular "one representing David – which is reported to be his own portrait – with long locks reaching to the shoulders, as was the custom of those times; it is so vivacious and so fresh in colouring that it seems to be living flesh, and there is armour on the breast, and on the arm with which he is holding the severed head of Goliath". An engraving by Wenceslas Holler (1650) shows the picture as described by Vasari – Only later – although not much later, as a copy (Madrid, Prado) by Teniers the Younger, which is similar to the present engraving, proves – the lower part was cut away and has disappeared. In 1648 the work belonged to Jan and Jacob van Verle of Antwerp [Ridolfi]; in 1737 it belonged to the Duke of Brunswick, recorded in his catalogue [1776] as a self-portrait by Raphael. Later it was attributed to Dosso. It was not until 1908 that Justi pointed out its connection with the quotation from Vasari. It is in all probability an original Giorgione. Wickhoff, Hermanin, Richter, Fiocco, Morassi and Coletti all agree that it is; and in any case accept it as a work of high quality and great fascination. A recent X-ray examination has shown beneath the face traces of a Madonna and Child in Giorgione's style: this strengthens the opinion that this is an original Giorgione. However, L. Venturi, Longhi and Pallucchini take it for a copy; Berenson for a Palma Vecchio.

## 27 ⊞⊕ 70×100 ▤⫶
### Christ Bearing the Cross
Venice, Scuola di S. Rocco
Vasari, in his first [1550] and second [1568] edition of the Vite states that Giorgione "worked on a picture of Christ bearing the Cross, with a Jew dragging him along, which in time was placed in the Church of S. Rocco, and today, through the veneration that many feel for it, it works miracles, as all may see". Nevertheless, this historian, in the second edition of his biographies, writes, à propos of Titian: "For the Church of S. Rocco, after these paintings, he made a picture of Christ with the Cross on his back and a Jew pulling him along with a cord, and this figure, which many thought was by the hand of Giorgione . . ." Vasari's uncertainty is reflected in modern criticism, for L. Venturi, Berenson, Richter, Coletti and Della Pergola

incline to Giorgione, while Morassi thinks it is a Titian and Fiocco a work of collaboration. Much has been said about its bad condition but in actual fact it seems almost unharmed: the artist's original brush strokes are clearly visible. L. Venturi affirms that the face of Christ, in its incomparable humanity and delicacy, seems to be one of Giorgione's most inspired creations.

## 28 ▦⊕ 75×66 ▤⫶
### Portrait of an Antiquarian
Formerly in London, Lansdowne Collection
Recently reproduced by Salvini ["P" 1961] as an

30

original, alongside the Christ Bearing the Cross at Venice (n.27), with Nordic elements derived from Schongauer, Dürer, Bosch and Memling.

## 29 ▦⊕ 76×63 ▤⫶
### Dead Christ Supported by an Angel
New York, Private collection
Michiel [1530] describes as follows a painting he saw in Gabriele Vendramin's house in Venice: "The dead Christ upon the sepulchre, with an angel who supports him, painted by the hand of Zorzo da Castelfranco, and re-worked by Titian". After many unacceptable identifications (one, in particular, related to the Pietà in the Savings Bank of Marca Trevigiana at Treviso, more properly ascribed to Florigerio but sometimes believed to be by Francesco Vecellio), Pallucchini ["AV" 1959–60] drew attention to the important picture under discussion, stating that it came from the Vendramin Palace and had recently gone to America.

This scholar accepted Michiel's statement that it was finished by Titian and this opinion is shared by Voss, while Coletti is inclined to see in it Giorgione's hand alone. X-ray has revealed an earlier use of the canvas (linen of fine weave) on which – diagonally across the present composition – the face of a young man is visible, similar to that in the Hampton Court picture (n.15) and also not unlike the present angel.
In the Pinacoteca Tadini at Lovere there is a derivative (formerly thought to be from an original by Verga) probably attributable to Pietro della Vecchia.

33

## 30 ⊞⊕ 84×69 ▤⫶
### Two Women and a Man (Trio; The Appeal)
Detroit, Institute of Arts
On the back of the canvas in old writing: "Fra Sebastiano del Piombo, Giorzon, Tizian". The subject has not been explained. The work passed from the Schönborn of Pommersfelden Collection (where Mündler ["K" 1867] ascribed it to Cariani, as did Cavalcaselle, Morelli [1891] and Berenson [1894]) to that of the Grand Duke of Oldenburg (and then A. Venturi [1900] ascribed it to Sebastiano del Piombo, as did Schmidt-Degener [1906] and Benkard [1908], while Borenius [1913] went back to Cariani, as did L. Venturi [1913], Fiocco [1941] and Pallucchini [1945], who rejected Morassi's opinion [1942] that it was by Palma Vecchio). The threefold artistic paternity mentioned in the above-mentioned writing was accepted by Valentiner ["BDI" 1925–26], Schubring ["AA" 1926], Suida [1935] and others. In reality the woman's figure on the left clearly shows Titian's characteristics, so different from those apparent in the woman opposite which are typical of Sebastiano del Piombo. Comparison with the altarpiece of S. Giovanni Crisostomo makes this clear. If the technique and the very spirit of these two painters are so obvious there is no reason to doubt Giorgione's hand in the male figure in the centre. Here we have an example of how Giorgione painted in his

final years and of his way of treating figures in full length.

## 31 ⊞⊕ 92×133 ▤⫶
### Madonna and Child between Two Saints
Madrid, Prado
It is agreed that St Roch is the saint on the right, painted with his unmistakable canonical attributes; the other saint is probably St Anthony of Padua because of the lily, although he has sometimes been taken for St Francis of Assisi. About 1650 the picture was offered by the Duke of Medina, Viceroy of Naples, to Philip II of Spain, and Velázquez himself – one may imagine – installed it in the Escorial sacristy from where it was transferred to its present position. Cavalcaselle attributed it to Francesco Vecellio, and Schmidt to Titian; Justi was the first to suggest Giorgione, followed by Morelli, A. Venturi, Berenson, Richter, Gamba [1954], Coletti, von Baldass and others. L. Venturi, on the other hand, from 1913, and Longhi, Suida, Fiocco, Morassi and Pallucchini agreed with Schmidt. Giorgione's pervasive charm spreads over

the picture ("That inward concentration of each figure, that trance-like suspension of movement, that silence all express Giorgione's feeling" [Gamba]; Fiocco, however, perhaps with more justice, is aware of the new, more self-assured and triumphant feeling of Titian; nor are the painting's similarities with the Gipsy Madonna in Vienna, now attributed to Titian, limited merely to iconographic details.

## 32 ⊞⊕ 80×64 ▤⫶
### Knight of Malta
Florence, Uffizi
According to Boehn [1908], Stefano Colonna is the man portrayed. On the back of the canvas there is an old inscription: "Giorgio da Castelfranco called Giorgione". It was bought [1654] as a work by Titian from Paolo del Sera by Cardinal Leopoldo de' Medici and through him it reached the Uffizi. Cavalcaselle attributes it to an anonymous follower of Giorgione's; Mündler to Pietro della Vecchia. Morelli [1880] suggested Giorgione and among the many scholars who agree are Berenson, Richter, A. Venturi, Fiocco (who compares it with the S. Rocco Christ Bearing the Cross in Venice [n.27]), Coletti and, lastly, L. Venturi [1954]. (He dates it c. 1508.) L. Venturi had at first maintained that it was by Titian, as did Suida, Morassi (who pointed out its similarity to the so-called Ariosto in the National Gallery of London), Pallucchini [1953], Salvini [1954] etc. Longhi [1946] thought it might be by Paris Bordone. Its state of preservation and the oxidisation of the colours prevent any accurate judgment; yet the general composition and the drawing reveal Titian's manner before 1515 when the artist was under Giorgione's influence. ("Giorgione's melancholy is here given expression by the proud bearing of the knight and the strong contrasts between light and shade" [Salvini].)

## 33 ⊞⊕ 108×122 ▤⫶
### Concert
Florence, Pitti Palace
This may be the picture Ridolfi saw [1648] in Paolo del Sera's picture gallery in Venice, from where – if Ridolfi's identification is correct – Cardinal Leopoldo de' Medici was to buy it. In any case he became its owner in 1654 and it passed to the Pitti from this prelate's collection. In the Medici Collection it was accepted as a work by Giorgione and continued to be ascribed to him until Morelli suggested that it was by Titian, and most

32

**34**

scholars agreed, from
A. Venturi [1928] to Suida,
Berenson, Morassi, Tietze,
Longhi, Coletti, Delogu, Della
Pergola, Valcanover [1960].
Cavalcaselle, on the other
hand, retained the original
attribution, followed by Justi
and, recently, by Fiocco
[1948] and L. Venturi [1954].
Richter [1937] took up an
intermediate position, thinking
that the work was begun
by Giorgione (the figure of the
young man on the left) and
finished by Titian; an
hypothesis shared, though
with reserve, by Pallucchini.
Tietze-Conrat ["GBA" 1955]
supported the attribution to
Sebastiano del Piombo
proposed by Hourticq and
accepted by Freedberg. Von
Hadeln, on the contrary,
supported the attribution to
Campagnola, already put
forward by Morelli [1880]
and repeated by Wickhoff.
The problem is complicated.
The deep understanding of the
human lot apparent in the face
of the harpsichord player –
a genuinely dramatic spirituality
– seems to go beyond
Giorgione's sphere of
achievement to a world of
more intense emotions,
suggested rather than
expressed, a world more
associated with Titian than
with Giorgione and which may
indicate an early work of
Titian rather than a widening
of Giorgione's scope. As for
the young man with the
plumed cap, he is not only
similar to Giorgione's work but
also much less well painted
than the other two figures.
It is almost superfluous to set
forth another accusation in
addition to the many which

subject which this scholar
includes among the four
"stories" about the prophet's
life commissioned by Alvise da
Sesti from Giorgione in 1508,
according to a contract
published by Molmenti.
Richter rightly throws doubt on
this document's authenticity.
Ruhemann's restoration carried
out in 1955 has revealed that
the halo round the head of
the presumed Daniel is in the
form of a cross, thus proving
that this figure is Christ and
that therefore the title given
above fits the scene depicted.
Moreover in a letter of 1612
to the Duke of Mantua
[Luzio, *La Galleria dei Gonzaga*,
1913], Camillo Sordi mentions
a picture by Giorgione of an
*Adulteress* in Venice; a
similar picture is mentioned
(1656) in Michele Spietra's
house, also in Venice; another,
certainly smaller in size than
the one now in Glasgow, was
found (1661) in the collection
of Gianvincenzo Imperiale in
Genoa [Luzio]; another was
reported in the possession of
the Pesaro brothers in Venice
[Sansovino, *Venetia*, 1663
(ed. Martinioni)]; finally in
1672, writing to Ciro Ferri
about an *Adulteress* in
Florence, Livio Meo asserts:
"if it is not a Giorgione then
it is a Titian".
  The Glasgow *Adulteress*
was in the possession of
Christina of Sweden (1689)
and was then attributed to
Giorgione; soon after (1721)
to Pordenone, but when it
went to Glasgow (1856) it
was as a Giorgione. Cavalcaselle [1871] expressed
doubts about its being by him.
Bernardini [1908] suggested
Sebastiano del Piombo.
L. Venturi [1913], Coletti,
Della Pergola and, at first,
Berenson ["GBA" 1926]
agreed. A. Venturi [1928] put
forward Romanino's name;
and the writer [1955],
tentatively, that of Domenico
Mancini. Meanwhile the
traditional attribution to the
master of Castelfranco found
favour with Bode, Morelli
[1880], Cook [1900], Justi,
Richter, Hendy [1954] and
Berenson himself ["AV" 1954],
who had earlier thought it was
a Titian ["AA" 1928; and
1936]; that is to say they
accept Longhi's opinion [1927],
which is shared by Suida,
Fiocco [1941], Morassi,
Pallucchini [1944], Gamba
[1954] and Valcanover [1960].
Its quality is high enough to
justify its inclusion in the
Giorgione-young Titian
problem. The dramatic

character of the composition
and certain affinities, not only
of iconography, with Titian's
frescoes in the Scuola del
Santo in Padua encourage one
to think that it might be by
him: yet an attribution to
Titian cannot be accepted with
absolute certainty because the
*Adulteress* reveals weaknesses
in the composition and in the
quality of the painting. Some
of the present appearance of
the picture may be due to
damage. It is difficult to credit
such harsh colours as coming
from Titian's palette. If not an
original Titian, the picture could
be a copy, carried out possibly

**35** (Plates LVIII–LXII)

by a contemporary artist. We
retain our attribution to
Mancini, a painter in the
Giorgione tradition who has
remained obscure, although
worthy of consideration.
E. Carli, as he has informed
me, arrived independently at
a similar conclusion.
  In the Accademia Carrara
of Bergamo there is a copy
(canvas 149 × 219) containing
an additional figure (of a
soldier) on the right hand side.
Berenson [1928] traced a
fragment of this figure
(size 54.5 × 43.5) to New
York (Sachs Collection, now
on loan to the National
Gallery, London). E. Camesasca
has drawn attention to another
unfinished copy showing the
bust of the adulteress and
those of the two men at
her side, in the possession of
Baron Donnafugata at Ragusa
(1960). According to him,
it shows characteristics similar
to those of Sebastiano del
Piombo. Other copies, in most
cases dating from much later,
are in private collections.

The golden light of the setting
sun shines on the group of
young people, while the
sounds of music recently
ended still echo; far off,
beneath a group of large trees,
is a shepherd with his flock;
in the background a distant
landscape fades into the sky.
In 1671 this famous painting
came into the possession of
Louis XIV. It is attributed to a
number of artists. Waagen
[1839] rejected the traditional
attribution to Giorgione in
favour of Palma Vecchio, but
Morelli [1880] claimed that it
was by Giorgione, while
Cavalcaselle [1871] was

inclined to think it was by an
imitator of Sebastiano del
Piombo. L. Venturi [1913],
at first also attributed it to
Sebastiano del Piombo; but
A. Venturi [1928] favoured
Giorgione, as did Berenson
[1932], Justi [1936], Gronau
["BA" 1936–37], Cook,
Richter, Fiocco [1941] and –
it appears – Coletti. (On
second thoughts L. Venturi
[1954] decided that the
painting was by Giorgione
carried out during his last
years. After Lafenestre's
suggestion [1909], more fully
developed by Springer and,
more authoratively still, by
Hourticq [1919] (who all
thought they saw in the picture
similarities to the *Nudes*
painted by Titian about 1530
for the Gonzagas), Titian's
name was taken up and was
accepted by Longhi [1927
and 1946], Suida, Morassi,
the present writer [1955] and
by others, including Valcanover
[1960]. On the other hand
Giorgione's touch is so evident
that Pallucchini himself [1953]
suggests that it could be a
work planned and sketched
by the master of Castelfranco
and carried out, after his death,
under Titian's supervision. The
soundness of the colour
impasto, the freedom in the
relationship between the
figures and the conception of
the landscape seem to have
some connection with Titian.

**36** 🏛 ⊕ 62×77 🗂 ⋮

**The Three Ages of Man**
Florence, Pitti Palace
This painting was first
mentioned when it was in
Prince Ferdinand's collection,
listed under the Lombard
School. It was later attributed

*(Above) Copy of painting
n.34 (Accademia Carrara,
Bergamo).*
*(Below) Fragment relating to
the Glasgow painting (n.34).*

have been moved to the work
since in all probability it will
be seen with new eyes after
restoration.

**34** 🏛 ⊕ 137×180 🗂 ⋮

**Christ and the Adulteress**
Glasgow, Corporation Galleries
Tietze-Conrat ["AB" 1945]
suggests that the theme of
this picture is the prophet
Daniel announcing the
innocence of Susannah, a

**35** 🏛 ⊕ 110×138 🗂 ⋮

**Fête Champêtre**
Paris, Louvre

**36** (Plates LXIII–LXIV)

**37**

**38**

**39**

**40**

to Lotto by Inghirami [1832], and Cavalcaselle concurred; Gronau [1895] suggested instead Morto da Feltre, and Berenson [1932] a "Master of the Three Ages", perhaps identifiable with the eighty-year-old Giovanni Bellini (to whom Longhi [1927] definitely attributed it). Richter was in favour of P.M. Pennacchi, and Fiocco tentatively suggested Torbido Meanwhile Cook, Suida and Morassi unanimously agreed with Morelli that it is a Giorgione, and Morassi has pointed out the originality of the composition, exquisitely Giorgionesque, in his opinion, in the moving silence brooding over the three men. The problem involves a whole group of painters from Giovanni Bellini to the followers of Giorgione; and if, at the Giovanni Bellini exhibition in Venice (1949), the work appeared to solve "one of the most impassioned problems concerning authorship in the history of art criticism" [Pallucchini, 1949], it must be remembered that even A. Venturi [1928] had been unable to suggest any artist to whom he could definitely attribute the painting and had to content himself with a general ascription to an unknown sixteenth-century Venetian. With equal uncertainty it was once more exhibited in 1955. However, with the caution necessitated by the bad state of preservation due to the layers of oxidised varnish which obscure the painting, one must admit that the most convincing hypothesis is that it is by Bellini.

**37** 🏢 ⊕ 76×99 ▤ ⋮
**The Concert**
Hampton Court, Royal Collection
The painting underwent the same vicissitudes in regard to its attribution to Giorgione as the previous work. In old Royal Catalogues it is given as Giorgione; then it was attributed to Lotto, to Morto da Feltre (Coletti seems to have accepted this in the end) and to Giovanni Bellini.

*(On the left) The three versions of painting n.41; (from the top) the paintings in Naples, Bowood and Bassano.*

*In painting n.38 a small opening has been made corresponding with the curve made by the lower outline of the hat and that of the left shoulder, so that one can see the head discovered in 1953 and here reproduced (turned 90° in an anti-clockwise direction).*

(Bottari makes no mention of it even in his most recent monograph on Giovanni Bellini [1963], nor for that matter does he mention the Pitti painting of the *Three Ages of Man*.) Morassi thinks it belongs to Giorgione's school, as did A. Venturi [1928], though when

comparing it with the *Three Ages of Man* he points out several stylistic discrepancies. Coletti, in agreement about this, suggests, as does Cook, a comparison between this *Concert* and the *Master with a Pupil* formerly in the Cook Collection, sometimes ascribed to Giorgione. The similarities with the Pitti *Three Ages of Man* are so numerous that one can assume the two paintings are by the same hand, perhaps by Bellini in his old age. Here, too, thick oxidised varnishes prevent valid judgment.

**38** 🏢 ⊕ 102×78 ▤ ⋮
**Young Man (The Impassioned Singer)**
Rome, Borghese Gallery
This portrait and the next one formed part of the same composition, which a document dated 15 March 1569 [in Rava, "NAV" 1920] records in Gabriele Vendramin's Collection in Venice: "a picture by the hand of Zorzon da Castelfranco with three large heads of singers"; but the catalogue of the Vendramin Collection compiled in 1627 [in Borenius, *The Picture Gallery of Andrea Vendramin*, 1923] makes no mention of the "large heads". As Cardinal Scipione Borghese was in touch with Francesco Vendramin in 1618–19, Della Pergola ["PA" 1954] has suggested that during 1627 the latter had arranged that the painting should be given to the prelate; an arrangement perhaps confirmed by other historical considerations. Della Pergola, moreover, thinks that the picture was already cut by the time it arrived in Rome; so that a third figure, probably of a woman, must have been lost. The picture in question and its twin (n.39) remained in

the possession of the Borghese family from the end of 1650, recorded by Manilli as "Giorgione's Two Jesters"; a description and attribution repeated in the inventory of 1693 and in successive ones until the deed of bequest of 1833, in which they are attributed to Giovanni Bellini. A. Venturi [Catalogue, 1893], entitling them "Caricatures of a Man", ascribed them to Domenico Capriolo, a name again mentioned recently by Fiocco (see below). Longhi, who in 1927 ["VA"] inclined to Mancini, in 1945 [in Della Pergola, 1954] put forward the opinion that they were by Giorgione. Della Pergola accepted this and, more specifically, said that the paintings dated from Giorgione's last years, shortly before 1510. This attribution, immediately adopted by L. Ferrara ["NA" 1954], was discussed in a kind of referendum arranged by "Scuola e Vita" [1954] when Fiocco supported Capriolo's name, as did Berenson; while Longhi himself, Grassi, Zeri and Wittgens pronounced in favour of Giorgione. Gnudi did not take up any definite stand but drew attention to the high quality of the pictures and their importance for Lombard painting (in particular that of Brescia). Moreover Valsecchi [*Venetian Painting*, 1954] and Collobi-Ragghianti ["VI" 1954] supported Della Pergola's thesis. Gamba [1954] was in favour of a provincial painter in the following of Pordenone; as was Coletti, who also suggested possible links with Savoldo and, more certainly, with Dosso Dossi. According to L. Venturi the two canvases date from after Giorgione's death; and Morassi, Pallucchini and Lombardo Petrobelli [1966] are against attributing them

**43**

**51**

**44**

**45**

42

46 AC

46 BD

47

48 A

48 B

49

50

53

52

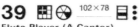

to Giorgione himself. As we have already said [1955] even if Della Pergola is right in identifying the Vendramin picture with the Borghese painting of the "large heads", one cannot necessarily accept without discussion the validity of a document of 1569, that is, of a period when Giorgione's name was already passing into legend. Finally, if one recognises the considerable power of the invention combined with interest in the human figure as shown in unpublished "preliminary sketches" attributed by various historians of the sixteenth century (in particular Vasari) to Giorgione, it would be difficult to deny, except with the greatest caution, that the work bears his characteristic stamp. The two paintings, which had probably been cleaned before, and which were summarily treated in 1945, were restored by A. Esposti (1953). This resulted, in particular, in the removal of retouchings in the background, and brought to light a three-quarters view head, sometimes considered a *pentimento*, but more probably indicating that the canvas had been used before.

Two copies from the Donà dalle Rose Collection of the paintings came on the market in Rome in 1937, attributed by Fiocco [1929] to Domenico Capriolo.

## 39 ⊞ ⊕ 102×78 ▤ ⦂
### Flute Player (A Cantor)
Rome, Borghese Gallery
For all information see the preceding entry.

## 40 ⊞ ⊕ 86×70 ▤ ⦂
### The Mocking of Samson(?)
Milan, Mattioli Collection
A pamphlet in the Marciana Library in Venice (Misc. 1,841, pamphlet N.15) enumerates among the paintings bequeathed by a certain Nicolò Renieri: "a picture by Giorgione da Castelfranco in which Samson is painted, his face half turned away and one hand leaning on a stone. He is shown grieving over his shorn head of hair and there are two figures laughing." The description corresponds with the subject of this painting which Longhi [in a private communication, 1946] ascribed with confidence to Giorgione. It would have been painted towards the end of his life, not only because of the technique which links the present picture with the two in the Borghese Gallery (see n.38 and n.39) but also because of the texture which, according to Boschini [1664], Giorgione achieved in his later years by means of "brush-strokes which give the impression of flesh and blood, but in a soft and natural manner . . ." Longhi's opinion, shared by Tschmelitsch [*Harmonia est discordia concors*, 1966] was opposed by L. Venturi [in Zampetti, 1955] who maintained that

the picture is later than Giorgione.

## 41 ⊞ ⊕ 1508-10? ▤ ⦂
### Shepherd with a Flute
According to one tradition the sitter is Antonello, Prince of Salerno, painted in shepherd's dress. This subject is known in at least three versions: one (canvas, 50 × 37) in the Gallerie Nazionali di Capodimonte in Naples; another (paper on wood, 48.3 × 36.8) in the Marquis of Lansdowne's collection at Bowood (Wiltshire); a third (canvas, 53 × 39.8) privately owned at Bassano. The painting in Naples, attributed by Berenson to Cariani, was more credibly ascribed to Sebastiano del Piombo by Morassi; the second one is usually attributed to Savoldo, though Longhi thought that it, too, was by Sebastiano del Piombo; the last one, never previously reproduced, suggests by its quality that it may be the prototype of the series. In any case critics agree about the Giorgionesque character of the subject, even if relegating it to the master's following – for example Coletti who compares it with the Borghese pictures (see n.38 and 39).

# Other works attributed to Giorgione

## 42 ⊞ ⊕ 51,5×40 ▤ ⦂
### St Mary Magdalen
Milan (?), Private collection
Included in the Giorgione exhibition (Venice, 1955) on the strength of Longhi's suggestion, supported by Fiocco and Suida, that it may be the earliest of Giorgione's paintings to have come down to us. According to this scholar, the artist based it on a work by Carpaccio. The attribution was rejected by L. Venturi and no other critic mentions it.

## 43 ⊞ ⊕ 69×121,5 ▤ ⦂
### The Legend of Romulus and Remus
Frankfurt, Städelsches Kunstinstitut
Discovered by Swarzenski ["FZ" 1937] and by Schwarzweller ["P" 1938], who ascribed it to Giorgione. The museum, too, backed this opinion even after cleaning had revealed not only the poor state of the picture but large unfinished areas. Coletti, although rejecting Giorgione as the painter, thought it had similarities with the two pictures in the Uffizi (n.1 and 2) painted when the artist was very young. Richter considered it a work from Giorgione's studio; Fiocco that it might be by Giulio Campagnola and Morassi that it might be by Catena.

## 44 ⊞ ⊕ 59×48 ▤ ⦂
### Homage to a Poet (?)
London, National Gallery
The rather obscure theme has given rise to various hypotheses; at first that it might be David teaching a devout follower or Solomon with some servants; Wickhoff [1895] connected it with a passage in Herodotus in which Aristagoras of Miletus tries to persuade Cleomenes, King of Sparta, to support the Ionian revolt; Cook [1907] proposed "The Golden Age" as its title, but most critics are inclined to think that it is an allegory—the exaltation of lyricism in the person of an ideal poet without any definite reference to anyone.

The painting may have come from the Villa Aldobrandini in Rome; between 1800 and 1801 it belonged to A. Day who sold it (1833) to the White Collection, from which it passed (1872) to that of H. Bohn. The National Gallery, where it now is, bought it from him [1885].

The attribution to the Master is by no means general. It was first supported by A. Venturi (*Galleria Crespi*, 1900) who later abandoned it. Justi and

*David Teniers the Younger, copy (c. 1660) of painting n.52 (Loeser Collection, formerly in Florence).*

Cook, likewise, started by supporting it and then rejected it in favour of an attribution to the school as adopted by the majority of critics. In point of fact only Morassi continues to believe in "an intimate relationship" between this picture and Giorgione, while at the National Gallery itself it is ascribed to an imitator of the master's early work.

## 45   65×76
**Landscape with Soldiers**
Milan, Private collection
The suggestion that it is by Giorgione [in A. Minghetti, *Quadro inedito di Giorgione* . . ., Pavia, undated] has found no support.

54

## Stories of Damon and Thyrsis

This type of subject, frequently found in classical literature, derives in the present instance from an eclogue by Tebaldeo. The four scenes, grouped as two pairs, (45 × 19.7) passed, it seems, from the Manfrin Collection in Venice to that of Da Porto di Schio (Vicenza); in 1936 they were acquired by Podio (Venice) and were sold to the National Gallery, London, in the following year. Clark reproduced them ["BM" 1937] as by Giorgione; but Borenius [*ibid.*] immediately attributed them to Palma Vecchio. Richter [*ibid.* 1938] suggested Previtali, as have all later critics.

## 46   20×18,5
A. **Damon Laments his Unrequited Passion**
B. **Thyrsis Asks Damon the Causes of his Grief.**
C. **Damon's Suicide**
   The painting is on the same panel as n.46 A
D. **Thyrsis Finds the Body of Damon**
   The painting is on the same panel as n.46 B.

## 47   50×39
**Christ Carrying the Cross**
Boston, Isabella Stewart Gardner Museum
It was bought by the Museum (1898) as a work by Giorgione, on the advice of Berenson; it was then attributed [Hendy, Catalogue, 1931] to Palma Vecchio as a derivative from a picture of the same subject by Giovanni Bellini in the Accademia dei Concordi at Treviso; today it is usually ascribed, and correctly, to Bellini himself.

## 48   45×66
A. **The Finding of Paris**
Milan, Gerli Collection
Transferred from panel to new-born Paris can be compared with that in n.50. It was found, together with the *pendant* (n.48 B) in the Albarelli Collection (Verona), attributed to Carpaccio; later it belonged to the Duke of Osuna; whence (1952), through a picture dealer in St Jean de Luz, it passed to the Gerli Collection. Cook reproduced it [1904] as Giorgione. Monneret de Villard, Conway [1925], Swarzenski ["FZ" 1937] and Schwarzweller ["P" 1938] agreed. Phillips [1937] and Richter are uncertain. L. Venturi [1913] attributed it to L. Bastiani; Gronau [1908], and later Morassi, canvas. The figure of the to Catena; while Fiocco and Coletti suggest Giulio Campagnola.

B. **Paris Handed over to a Nurse**
Milan, Gerli Collection
A *pendant* of the above (see 48 A for all information).

61

62

## 49   29,5×47
**Landscape with Figures**
Paris, Lebel Collection
Transferred to canvas from panel. Reproduced by Morassi [1942] as a youthful work by Giorgione, perhaps in partnership with Catena. It can be compared with the two Gerli canvases (n.48 A and B). Coletti disagrees.

## 50   38×56,5
**Paris Abandoned on Mount Ida ( ? )**
Princeton, University Art Museum
Mather ["AB" 1927], and later Conway, Richter, De Batz, Morassi (but with doubts), Della Pergola, Coletti and others attribute this painting to Giorgione. Until 1957 Berenson thought it was a copy of a lost painting by Giorgione, and Fiocco ascribes it to a follower.

## 51   50×60
**The Return of Judith**
Milan, Rasini Collection
Coletti considered it a work of Giorgione's youth [*Pittura Veneta del '400*, 1953], and subsequently he repeated this opinion [1955], but no other scholar took up the idea.

## 52   91×63
**The Finding of Paris**
Budapest, Szépművészeti Muzeum
Michiel [1525] wrote that in Taddeo Contarini's house "The picture of a landscape representing the new-born Paris and two shepherds

63

standing nearby was by the hand of Zorzo da Castelfranco and was one of his earliest works." An engraving of the complete picture was reproduced by Van Kassel (1659) in *Theatrum Pictorium*, and Teniers the Younger made a copy of it in oils when he was working in the picture gallery of Leopold Archduke of Austria in Brussels. After that all trace of it disappeared. The painting in Budapest showing only a fragment with the two figures on the right belonged in the nineteenth century to the patriarch Pyrker in Venice. Morelli, Justi and others — including Morassi, although he was doubtful — considered it a Giorgione, but most modern scholars — Fiocco and Berenson among them — believe it to be a copy. It is not in a good state of preservation, particularly because of overpainting, and this makes a decision difficult.

65

## 53   8×55
**The Adoration of the Magi**
Dublin, National Gallery of Ireland
Bought in Rome in 1856. Now generally rejected as a Giorgione, but still attributed to him in the Dublin gallery.

## 54   13,2×27,6
**Landscape and a Youth (A Young Page)**
Bergamo, Suardo Collection
From the Abati Collection in Bergamo, where it was ascribed to Giorgione. Frizzoni and Fiocco accepted this opinion. Lauts [*Carpaccio*, 1962] attributed it to Carpaccio, as did Muraro [1966], the present writer [1966] and Perocco [1967]. In favour of this is the existence of a drawing for the figure of the boy (Leningrad, Hermitage) altogether in Carpaccio's style. L. Venturi's opinion [1957] attributing it to Lotto has little to be said for it. According to Morassi, until 1939 the work formed part of the decoration of a piece of furniture, with two similar little paintings, illustrating, perhaps, Ceres and Abundance.

## 55   12×19
**Leda and the Swan**
Padua, Museo Civico
This forms part of a series, including the *Country Idyll* in the same museum and the *Old Man*

55

56

57

58

59

60

66

67

68

69

72

*with an Hour-Glass and a Woman Playing a Viola* in Washington (n.56 and 57) which Coletti thinks comes "from the home of the Counts of Falier in Asolo" (see n.58) and once formed part of a fine piece of furniture, perhaps a jewel cabinet. In any case this painting and the

following one came to the Padua museum in 1864 through the Legate Emo Capodilista. They are thought to be by Giorgione. Cook [1900] was the first to put forward his name, and Conway [1929], Moschetti [1938], Fiocco, Morassi, Longhi [in Pallucchini, 1946], Coletti, Grossato [1957] and others — including, originally [1955] the present writer — think them genuine. Opinion varies about their date. Morassi and others believe they were painted at the end of the fifteenth century or the beginning of the sixteenth, and Fiocco suggests 1505. Pallucchini [1947] is doubtful and at first agreed with Gronau [1908] that the picture was by Giulio Campagnola. Justi [1908] and L. Venturi [1913 and 1926] favour an imitator.

## 56 ⊞ ⊕ 12×19 ☰⦂
### Country Idyll
Padua, Museo Civico
The subject is not clear as is often the case with Giorgione and his circle. However the "motive" of the young woman with a child in her arms and the young man with flowers is in some ways reminiscent of the *Tempest* (n.16); and in fact Coletti thought that it anticipated this latter painting, although it could equally well have been based on it. The treatment is noticeably summary and is not, one must add, entirely satisfactory. Morassi says that this can be explained by its "essentially decorative" purpose. For all other information, see n.55.

## 57 ⊞ ⊕ 12×19 ☰⦂
### Old Man with an Hour-Glass and a Woman Playing a Viola
Washington, Phillips Memorial Gallery
It was transferred (1937) from the Pulszky Collection in Budapest to the St Luke Gallery in Vienna; from there to the von Thyssen Collection in Lugano and finally to its present position. Critics agree in connecting it with the two preceding paintings (see n.55 and 56).

## 58 ⊞ ⊕ 11×20 ☰⦂
### Venus and Cupid
Washington, National Gallery of Art (Kress Bequest)
It comes from the collection of the Counts Falier at Castelle d'Asolo; in 1939 it was bought by the S.H. Kress Foundation. In the catalogue of works [1941] it is compared with the three preceding small paintings (see n.55). De Batz [1942] agreed and Coletti inferred that all four paintings must originally have belonged to the Counts Falier. Morassi, on the other hand, thinks that *Venus and Cupid* was painted by Previtali and Berenson [1957] attributes it to a follower of Giorgione.

## 59 ⊞ ⊕ 28×39 ☰⦂
### Allegory of Chastity
Amsterdam, Rijksmuseum
The woman accompanied by

the traditional unicorn in the position established by the canons of iconography has been identified also as St Justina [Pallucchini, 1944]. The picture passed from the Buttery Collection in London to that of Kaufmann in Berlin; thence to the Lanz gallery in Amsterdam and from there to its present location. Bode suggested [1900] that it is by Giorgione and more recently Morassi and Coletti agreed. Fiocco [1941] was doubtful and Frizzoni [1904] thought it a copy of a lost painting by Giorgione; at the same time Monneret de Villard attributed it to Giorgione's school as did Justi [1908] and others, including Berenson [1957]. In Degenhart's opinion [1941] it is by a Ferrarese painter, although he does not feel certain about this. The bad condition of the painting prevents any sure judgment.

In a private collection in Venice there is a version of the same subject, but with a wider landscape beneath the setting sun, perhaps painted at the end of the fifteenth century: in any case it proves the existence of an important prototype.

## 60 ⊞ ⊕ 46×44 ☰⦂
### Landscape with a Young Mother and a Halberdier (Idyll)
Compton Wynyates, Warwickshire, Marquis of Northampton's Collection
Conway [1929] reproduced it as an early Giorgione. Fiocco and Coletti are of the same

64

73

opinion but Berenson rejects the attribution.

## 61 ⊞ ⊕ 44,5×34,3 ☰⦂
### Bust of a Young Woman
Hampton Court, Royal Collection
This probably comes from the collection of Charles I. Berenson [until 1957] thinks

it must be closely connected with the *Three Ages* in the Pitti (n.36) and an early Giorgione, but hardly any critics have agreed. It has been attributed to Bellini and Ercole de Roberti.

## 62 ⊞ ⊕ 72,5×54 ☰⦂
### Portrait of Vittore Cappello ( ? )
Budapest, Szépművészeti Muzeum
The sitter has often been

71

identified with Antonio Broccardo, on the strength of an inscription ("Antonius Brokardus Marii f.") on the parapet. It came to the collection of Pyrker, Patriarch of Venice, as a Titian and was accepted as such by Pulszky. Since then it has been attributed to many different

artists: — Francesco Morone [Mündler], Torbido [Frizzoni], B. Licinio [Ludwig; A. Venturi; von Fabriczy], Cavazzola [Loeser], Cariani [Morassi], Pordenone [Frimmel; Coletti]. Morelli ascribed it to Giorgione, followed with some reservations by Thausing, Berenson [until 1957], Cook Justi, Fiocco, Pallucchini, Gamba and Longhi. If, however, the portrait was painted in the second decade of the sixteenth century, it cannot be by Giorgione.

## 63 ⊞ ⊕ 68×55 ☰⦂
### Young Man with a Book (with a Small Volume of Petrarch's Poems; Onigo Portrait)
San Francisco, H.M. De Young Memorial Museum (Kress Bequest)
It comes from the family of Onigo of Treviso, hence its title "Onigo Portrait", although there is no proof that it represents any member of the family. It belonged to the antiquarian Volpi of Florence, then to the Cook Collection in Richmond and finally to the Kress Foundation of New York. For a long time it was attributed to Giorgione. Borenius [1913] followed by Morassi attributed it to Cariani: Fiocco proposed Pordenone and received a good deal of support, for example from Berenson (though with reservations), Coletti, Pallucchini [in Zampetti, 1955] etc.

## 64 ⊞ ⊕ 64×130 ☰⦂
### Apollo and Daphne
Venice, Patriarchal Seminary
Probably part of the decoration on the front of a marriage chest. According to von Hadeln [in Ridolfi, 1914] the panel must have been cut on the left, which bore the related episode of Apollo killing the serpent Python. Morelli's suggestion that it is by Giorgione was strongly supported by Berenson [1932, until 1957] although he regarded it as only partly by his hand. Cavalcaselle [1871] thought it was by Schiavone, as did L. Venturi. The present writer does not agree [1955]. Pallucchini [1946] sought to connect it with Paris Bordone. Recent cleaning (1954) has persuaded most art critics, including Pallucchini, that it may be a Titian, as the vivid colours and the dramatic vitality of the figures suggest.

78

## 65 ⊞ ⊕ 75×67 ▤ ⁝
**The Bravo**
Vienna, Kunsthistorisches Museum
According to Richter [1937], this picture can be identified with *Claudius Luscius attacking Celius Plotinus,* mentioned by Ridolfi [1648] as in a Venetian collection as a Giorgione. In 1659 it belonged to Archduke Leopold William of Austria, and the following year it was engraved as a Giorgione for the *Theatrum Pictorium;* this attribution remained unaltered until Cavalcaselle [1871] substituted Cariani, while Wickhoff proposed Palma Vecchio in agreement with L. Venturi and Berenson. Justi [1908] went back to the original attribution, followed – as has been said – by Richter, although with reservations. Meanwhile A. Venturi [1928] argued that

74

75

76

77

Dosso Dossi could be the artist; and Wilde connected it with the hypothetical "Master of the Self-Portrait" and Della Pergola attributed it to an unknown imitator of Giorgione; moreover, according to Berenson's hypothesis [until 1957] the painting is certainly a copy of a Giorgione painted by Palma Vecchio. But as early as 1927 Suida and Longhi recognised it as a Titian, as do most modern critics. Richter suggested that the head on the right (X-rays reveal that it was originally a clear profile [Wilde]), was repainted in the eighteenth century: in fact a copy drawn by Van Dyck [Adriani, 1941], appears exactly as in the X-ray photograph. There have been a number of versions, among which is one by Pietro della Vecchia in the Doria Gallery' in Rome.

## 66 ⊞ ⊕ 25×30 ▤ ⁝
**A Page**
Milan, Pinacoteca Ambrosiana
In the past the boy was thought to be Jesus as a child "with a ball in his hand". According to Wilde he is Paris holding the prize for the most beautiful goddess. Already by 1618 Cardinal Federico Borromeo had given it to the present gallery. Traditionally it was ascribed to Andrea del Sarto; then to Giorgione [in A. Ratti, *Guida . . . della Pinacoteca Ambrosiana,* 1907]; and finally to D. Mancini [Fiocco]. Coletti thinks it a copy of a lost Giorgione and perhaps this is the most convincing opinion; but Morassi seems inclined to think it by Giorgione himself.

## 67 ⊞ ⊕ 79×68 ▤ ⁝
**Portrait of a Young Man in a Fur, Holding a Sword**
New York, Frick Collection
From Tietze [1950] to Valcanover [1960], etc., it is usually, and correctly, attributed to Titian. Coletti alone thinks it by Giorgione.

## 68 ⊞ ⊕ 90×73 ▤ ⁝
**Knight with his Squire (Gattamelata Portrait)**
Florence, Uffizi
Cavalcaselle changed the traditional attribution to Giorgione in favour of Torbido; as did critics, with strong backing [Borenius; etc.], from Gamba to Cavazzola. Longhi [1946] re-attributed the painting to Giorgione, and Salvini [1954] accepted this, although with reservations. Coletti disagreed. Nevertheless, if not by Giorgione (because of the "rather metallic colours, the heaviness of the burnished parts, the rather hard, dry modelling", pointed out by Coletti) the picture could be an old copy of an original by the master himself.

## 69 ⊞ ⊕ 80×67,5 ▤ ⁝
**Double Portrait**
Rome, Museo di Palazzo Venezia
The concentrated and enigmatic thoughtfulness of the figure in the foreground forms

a contrast with the more open face of the young man behind, causing a subtle "lack of balance", accentuated by the vertical lines of the central column, while the gentle falling light contributes to the mysterious atmosphere of the whole. Ravaglia suggested, though no critic has taken it up, that the two men portrayed are the musicians Verdelot and Obreth (Verdelotto and Obretto). Longhi had little support for his attempt [1927 and 1946] to assign the painting to Giorgione's last years, just before the *Knight* in the Uffizi (n.68), only Coletti agreeing with him, while Berenson attributed the painting to D. Mancini.

## 70 ⊞ ⊕ 208×318 ▤ ⁝
**The Judgment of Solomon**
Kingston Lacy, (Dorset), Bankes Collection
Ridolfi [1648] mentions the existence of a *Judgment of Solomon* "with the figure of the priest unfinished" in the Grimani house at S. Marcuola in Venice. Some scholars have identified this with the present picture and have recognised it as the hand of Giorgione alone [Fiocco; Gamba] or with help (or completion) from Sebastiano del Piombo [Suida; Morassi] or from another painter [Berenson]. Others have suggested that it is by Stefano Cernotto, a follower of Pitati [Wickhoff], Catena [R. Fry], Titian [Hourticq] and Sebastiano del Piombo, unassisted [L. Venturi; Longhi; Pallucchini; Morassi; Coletti].

## 71 ⊞ ⊕ 50×45 ▤ ⁝
**Portrait of a Man (Ariosto)**
New York, Metropolitan Museum (Altman Collection)
Berenson – until 1957 – vigorously supported the attribution of this portrait to Giorgione. The Metropolitan Museum attributes it to him or to Titian, but recent critics do not think it is by either.

## 72 ⊞ ⊕ 73×64 ▤ ⁝
**Portrait of Francesco Maria della Rovere ( ?)**
Vienna, Kunsthistorisches Museum
Transferred from panel to canvas, Suida [1935] supports the identification given above, but Gronau thinks it is a portrait of Giovan Francesco Maria della Rovere. Suida himself suggests attributing it to Giorgione, but Morassi

*Copy of painting n.79 (Dresden, Gemäldegalerie).*

*Copies of painting n.81: the version in the Spanio Collection in Venice (on the left), and the version in the Howard Collection at Castle Howard (on the right).*

alone agrees and then only with reservations. Pallucchini [1944] favours Sebastiano del Piombo; other scholars, less convincingly, suggest Catena, while Cavalcaselle [1876] discerned Licinio's hand and Berenson [1932] that of Michele da Verona.

## 73 ⊞ ⊕ 360×406 ▤ ⁝
**St Mark, St George and St Nicolas save Venice from the Hurricane**
Venice, Accademia
The subject refers to a legendary episode of 1340; in the centre the ship belonging to the demons who have invoked the storm. On the right the ship of the saints who

will sink the demons. In the foreground more devils try to attack the patrons of Venice. The picture was formerly in the "hostel" of the Scuola Grande di S. Marco and came to the Accademia in 1829. Still in doubt is the question of chronology. Vasari attributed the painting first [1550] to Giorgione, then 1568 to Palma Vecchio; Sansovino [1581] also thought it was by Palma, although he mentioned that "others" attributed it to Paris Bordone; Boschini [1664] and Zanetti [1771] again ascribed it to Giorgione, but Lomazzo [1584], Scannelli [1657] and Sandrart [1675] returned to Palma. In the end the attribution to Giorgione prevailed, but Bordone's assistance was admitted, and Cavalcaselle – followed by Jacobsen [1899], Wickhoff [1904] and others – thought his help must have been considerable and also that there were subsequent additions, from a third painter. These hypotheses caused Justi – and von Hadeln [1909], Gronau [1911], Richter, etc. – to conclude that Palma Vecchio and Bordone collaborated in executing an idea of Giorgione's. Berenson was the first [1899] – agreeing

80

82

with Monneret de Villard, von Boehm [1908], Bercken [1927] etc. – to attribute to Paris Bordone the painting of the ship on the right and to suggest that the rest of the picture was by Giorgione. This idea was rejected by Schmidt [1908] who strongly supported a collaboration between Palma Vecchio and Paris Bordone. Most modern scholars, including L. Venturi, Morassi, Coletti and Berenson himself [1932, and until 1957], agree. To sum up, the Palma-Bordone association seems to be the most reasonable solution, taking into consideration that the work underwent alterations and restoration, as well as the insertion of the rectangle with the sea monster at the bottom left hand side where originally there was a doorway.

83

84

85

## 74    75 × 62,5

### Portrait of a Man
Washington, National Gallery of Art (Kress Bequest)
Formerly in the collections of H. Doetsch in London and Goldman of New York. Cook ascribed it [1906] to Giorgione An X-ray examination revealed two other versions beneath the present portrait: Borrough [1938] thought that all three were by Giorgione, but Richter – followed with hesitation by Morassi – considered him responsible only for the first version and thought that Titian had painted the other two. Meanwhile Berenson attributed the portrait to Palma Vecchio, and almost all present day scholars agree.

## 75    20 × 16

### Little Faun
Munich, Bayerische Staatsgemäldesammlungen
This painting has been known since 1781 when it was transferred from the Schleissheim Collection to the Hofgarten Gallery, from where it came to its present location. Morelli [1880] attributed it to Lotto: others have suggested Titian and Palma Vecchio [Morassi]. Longhi, in 1928, and again in 1946, ascribed it to Giorgione "because the picture shows the same 'gymnastic formula' as the frescoes of the Fondaco dei Tedeschi". Coletti among others rejected the idea, but Pignatti [1955] seems to accept it: and, indeed, of all the suggestions put forward it seems the most plausible.

## 76    65 × 74

### David with Goliath's Head
Vienna, Kunsthistorisches Museum
An engraving by L. Vorsterman the Younger (1660), made when the painting belonged – as a Pordenone – to the collection of Archduke Leopold William of Austria at Brussels and published in *Theatrum Pictorium*, shows that it was originally larger. Many students of Giorgione's work ignore it. Wilde [Museum Catalogue 1938] attributes it to an imitator; Morassi, while proposing to defer judgment until "after a thorough cleaning of the picture", suggested attributing it to Giorgione, a proposal strongly backed by Suida [1954], Coletti and, in part, by Berenson who thought it either an old copy or an original from Giorgione's last years (in any case it must be connected with this late period) though sadly spoiled by the "efforts at restoration in very early times", already noticed by Suida.

## 77    70 × 54

### Ceres
Berlin, Staatliche Museen
Transferred from panel to canvas. The attribution to Giorgione made by Zimmermann ["BRM" 1954], has not been accepted. Pallucchini thinks [in Coletti, 1955] it is by Sebastiano del Piombo; according to Coletti it could be by Gerolamo da Treviso the Younger.

## 78

### Witchcraft (The Horoscope)
Panel (132 × 192). The subject is somewhat obscure, although probably connected with magic. Formerly in the Dresden Picture Gallery (destroyed in 1945), and long ascribed to Giorgione, until Morelli suggested that it was a copy of a lost painting by him. A. Venturi, Berenson [until 1957], and others, including Coletti, agreed. L. Venturi and Swarzensky, perhaps rightly, rejected this indirect connection with Giorgione.

## 79    *55 × 70* ?

### The Judgment of Paris
Ridolfi [1648] attributes to Giorgione a picture in Leoni's house in S. Lorenzo in Venice illustrating the same subject, of which there exist – Coletti apparently agrees – unsigned copies: one (52.5 × 67.5) in the Dresden Picture Gallery, another (60 × 74) formerly in the Lanfranchi Collection of Chiavari, and others (Uffizi, Florence; Larpendt Collection, Oslo; etc.). Thought to be based on a conception of Campagnola's [Gronau] or of Titian's [Morassi], while L. Venturi prefers a late imitator.

## 80    70 × 54

### Young Man with a Fur
Munich, Bayerische Staatsgemäldesammlungen
On the back of the panel, perhaps in seventeenth-century handwriting, is written: "Giorgio de Castel Franco, F. Maestro de Tiziano". For a long time this was assumed to be the work mentioned by Vasari and Ridolfi (but wrongly, as Ragghianti points out [in Vasari], since the painting in question was of smaller dimensions and Vasari mentions it as being in his own "book" of drawings [see n.112]). But the *Young Man with a Fur* continued for a long time to be attributed to Giorgione, even after it went to Munich (1748), until Cavalcaselle [1871] attributed it instead to Palma Vecchio. Many present day scholars agree, including Berenson [until 1957], although admitting its derivation from a Giorgionesque original. On the other hand, Morelli thought it by Cariani, and A. Venturi [1928] by Mancini, although with reservations. Justi [1908] took up again Giorgione's authorship. Della Pergola suggested that it was by an unknown imitator who had also painted the *Bravo* (n.65). Ragghianti himself favours Titian.

## 81

### Boy and a Warrior
It has been recognised that Giorgione used the theme of the warrior and the boy in a painting which has never come to light but of which there are several derivatives. Cavalcaselle [1871] mentions five, all of small dimensions, tall and narrow and limited to the two figures: in the Kunsthistorisches Museum in Vienna (depot); in the Alfieri di Sostegno Collection, Turin; in the Carlisle Collection, Naworth Castle (Waagen noted it there [1854]), formerly in the Orléans Collection; in the Redern Collection, Berlin; and in the Landesmuseum, Stockholm. An X-ray photograph of this last picture shows that it has been painted over an early sixteenth-century *Deposition* and must definitely be ruled out as a possible prototype. Cavalcaselle rejected the Redern painting because it is signed by G. Pencz (later [cf. Frizzoni, "A" 1902] it went to the Kaufmann Collection). The Carlisle picture can be identified with the panel (21 × 18) now at Castle Howard, Yorkshire. Scholars including Justi, Berenson [until 1957] and Richter maintain that it is derived from a painting by Giorgione, while Coletti admits that it could even be by the master himself. Coletti also mentions ["E" 1955] a canvas (70 × 86.5), formerly belonging to Sebastiano Barozzi, subsequently in the Axel Palace and finally in the Spanio Collection, in Venice, in which the theme is treated in a horizontal format, with the addition of a helmet on a window sill. According to this scholar – and he says [1955] that Fiocco and Pallucchini share his opinion – "it is perhaps the original" This hypothesis was then dropped.

A portrait presumed to be of Gaston de Foix (18 × 14) formerly in Lord Northwick's collection attributed to Giorgione [Catalogue, 1864; and Borenius, 1921], came up for sale at Christie's (London, 1965) attributed to Pietro della Vecchia.

## 82    69 × 52

### Portrait of a Young Man
New York (?), Duveen Property
First recorded in the Eissler Collection, Vienna (c.1924), then Duveen, New York (1926), then Bache, also New York, and then again Duveen. Bode, in a private communication, was first to propose Giorgione; L. Venturi [1933] and Morassi apparently agreed, and Richter described it as an "extremely Giorgionesque" work. Suida [1922] attributed it to Titian. Other students of Giorgione ignore it.

## 83    124 × 65

### St George
Venice, Cini Collection
Formerly in London, first in Sir Andley Neeld's collection, then in Agnew's. Waagen was the first [1854] to attribute it to Giorgione; this suggestion was adhered to by L. Venturi [1954] and M. Calvesi [1956] when Borenius had already ascribed it to Palma Vecchio, backed by Fiocco and Gronau, but opposed by Spahn [1932]. Most recent scholars, beginning with Longhi [1936], are inclined to accept it as a Titian [Tietze; Morassi; Pallucchini; Valcanover, 1960], but do not agree about the date.

## 84    31,7 × 24,1

### Bust of a Woman (Portrait of a Lady; A Courtesan)
Fullerton, Norton Simon Foundation (Kress Collection)
In the nineteenth century it belonged to Prince Lichnowsky (Kuchelna), then to Lord Melchett (Romsey), and finally to Duveen, New York. In 1929, von Baldass attributed it to Cariani; but Suida, much more credibly, later suggested Titian, and Morassi, Pignatti [1955], Longhi [in Zampetti, 1955] and others agreed. Many art historians, nevertheless, prefer Giorgione: e.g. Gronau, Mayer [1932], Fischel, Richter, Tietze, Richardson, De Batz, Berenson [until 1957], Coletti, etc.

## 85    26 × 21,2

### Portrait of Matteo Costanzo ( ?)
New York, Private collection
It bears the date "MDX" and

*Engraving by Campagnola, possibly connected with painting n.97.*

the name of the sitter "MATHEUS CONSTANTIVS", although he died in 1504 (see n.12). Hourticq [1930] suggested it was by Giorgione and Mayer [1932] and L. Venturi were of the same opinion. Richter and Morassi think it from Giorgione's school; other critics ignore it.

## Other works mentioned in historical documents

Below is a list of other works of which there is now no trace but which were attributed to Giorgione in original documents or about whose identification with paintings in existence today art historians are not in unanimous agreement. As there are no references to the dates of execution the paintings are grouped according to the relevant sources, beginning with the earliest.

### Orders for Payment
(State Archives, Venice).
**86.** Painting for the Audience Hall in the Doge's Palace. (See *Outline Biography* 1507 and 1508.)

### Taddeo Albano
(Letter to Isabella d'Este.)
**87.** Two *Nativities*. See *Outline Biography* (1510) and, for the proposed identification with existing paintings, *Catalogue*, n.8 and 9.

## Marcantonio Michiel

*(Notizie di Opere del Disegno*, 1525–42*)*

**88. Aeneas and Anchises.** In Taddeo Contarini's house in Venice (1525); some scholars identify this with the *Tramonto* in London (*Catalogue*, n.18).

**89. The Birth of Paris.** In Taddeo Contarini's house in Venice (1525); see *Catalogue* n.52.

**90. Portrait of Gerolamo Marcello.** In the house of the sitter at S. Tomà, Venice (1525); see *Catalogue*, n.25.

**91. St Jerome Reading.** In Gerolamo Marcello's house in Venice (1525): "St Hieronimo who is reading, half-length portrait by the hand of Zorzi da Castelfranco". Mentioned by Ridolfi [1648] in Malipiero's house.

**92. Bust of a Warrior.** In the house of Giannantonio Venier in Venice [1528]: "The soldier in armour but without a helmet, half-length portrait, was by the hand of Zorzi da Castelfranco".

**93. Young Shepherd with a Fruit.** In Giovanni Ram's house in Venice, in Santo Stefano (1531): "The picture of the head of the young shepherd who holds a piece of fruit in his hand was by the hand of Zorzi da Castelfranco".

Michiel mentions another painting in the same house, usually identified with n.14 in the *Catalogue*.

**94. St James.** In Antonio Pasqualino's house in Venice (5 January 1532), a replica or copy which has some connection with our n.27: "The head of S. Jacomo with the pilgrim's staff was by the hand of Zorzi da Castelfrancho, or copied by one of his pupils from the painting of Christ in S. Rocho".

**95. St Jerome in the Desert.** In Andrea Oddoni's house in Venice (1532), a copy of an original by Giorgione: "The naked St Jerome sitting in a desert in moonlight by the hand of . . . copied from a painting by Zorzi da Castel-

**96. Naked Man in a Landscape.** In August 1543, Michele Contarini owned a drawing in Venice which is connected with a painting owned by Michiel himself: "the naked man in a landscape doing penance was by the hand of Zorzo . . . and is the nude which I have in a painting by this same Zorzo".

**97. Nude of a Woman.** In Pietro Bembo's house in Padua is a miniature by Giulio Campagnola of ". . . a nude woman drawn by Zorzo, reclining and with her face in profile". An etching by Campagnola in the Albertina Museum in Vienna is probably a copy of this same original drawing by Giorgione.

**98. Portrait of a Man.** Mentioned as being in Pietro Servio's house. In a note added to Michiel's text in a different hand in 1575: "A portrait of Zorzo da Castelfranco's father".

*Copy engraved by D. Cunego of painting n.138.*

140

## Paolo Pino

*(Dialogo di pittura*, 1548.)

**99. St George.** "[Giorgione] painted a picture of St George on foot and in armour leaning on the head of a lance with his feet on the very edge of a bright limpid stream in which he is reflected foreshortened to the top of his head, then Giorgione placed a mirror against a tree trunk which showed St George's whole figure back view and from one side. He then placed a second mirror so that it reflected St George from the other side."

From an iconographical point of view, if one wishes to see another example of a painting showing various "views" by means of mirrors, one must turn to Savoldo's *Gaston de Foix* in the Louvre in Paris. (See further on n.110.)

## Giorgio Vasari

*(Le vite*, 1550.)

**100. Paintings for Ca' Soranzo.** "[Giorgione] painted the entire façade of the Ca' Soranzo on the Piazza di S. Polo; wherein, besides many pictures and historical events and other fanciful stories there is a picture painted in oils on plaster, a work which has withstood rain, sun and wind, and has remained fresh until our own day." Ridolfi also refers to it [1648] but as having by then suffered much damage.

## Paris Bordone

(Catalogue of works in the house of Giovanni Grimani, 1563)

**101. A Nativity.** A "nativity (crèche) by the hand of Zorzi of Chastelfrancho for 10 ducats" [Fogolari, "AN" 1910]. Its identity with the Allendale *Nativity* (n.8) seems doubtful.

## Gabriele Vendramin

(See *Outline Biography*, 1567.)

**102. Two Figures.** In the "Chamber of Antiquities": "a small painting of two figures in chiaroscuro by the hand of Zorzon da Castelfranco".

## Giorgio Vasari

*(Le vite*, 1568[2])

**103. Bust of a Man with a Commander's Cap.** In the possession of Grimani, Patriarch of Aquileia: "A larger head, portrayed from life; the man holds in one hand the red cap of a commander and wears a fur mantle, beneath which appears one of those old-fashioned doublets . . ." Quoted by Ridolfi [1648] in van Verle's house in Antwerp.

**104. Head of a Cupid.** Owned by the same Grimani, the head "of a cupid . . . with fleecy hair".

**105. Portrait of Giovanni Borgherini with his Master.** In the possession of this Borgherini's sons in Florence: "the portrait of Giovanni as a youth in Venice, and in the same picture is the master who used to teach him: . . ."

**106. Bust of a Captain.** In Anton de' Nobili's house in Florence: "the head of a captain in armour . . . who is said to be one of the captains whom Consalvo Ferrante took with him to Venice . . ."

A painting illustrating the same subject, perhaps identifiable with this one, is attributed to Giorgione by Ridolfi [1648] who saw it in Senator Domenico Ruzzini's house in Venice.

**107. Portrait of Consalvo Ferrante.** "[Giorgione] painted [in Venice] the great Consalvo in armour, which was a very beautiful work . . . and Consalvo took it away with him." Also quoted by Ridolfi [1648].

**108. Portrait of Doge Leonardo Loredan.** Vasari relates that it was exhibited in Venice on the occasion of a Feast of the Ascension, according to the custom of the time. Ridolfi also mentions it [1648].

**109. Portrait of a Man.** In the house of the engraver Giovanni Bernardi at Faenza, a likeness of "his father-in-law".

**110. Male Nude, Back View.** "It is related that Giorgione, at the time when Andrea Verrocchio was making his bronze horse, fell into an argument with certain sculptors, who maintained, because sculpture showed various attitudes and aspects of a single figure by one walking round it, that therefore sculpture was superior to painting which could only show one figure in one position, or perhaps only a part of a figure. Giorgione was of the opinion that it was possible to show in a painted scene, without any necessity of walking round, at a single glance, all the various aspects that a man can present in many gestures – which sculpture cannot do except by a change of position and point of view, so that in the case of sculpture the points of view are many, and not one. Further, he

proposed to show in one painted figure the front, the back and the profile from both sides, an assertion which astonished his hearers; and he did it in the following way. He painted a naked man with his back turned to the spectator, at whose feet was a pool of very clear water, wherein he painted the reflection of the man's front; on one side was a burnished cuirass that he had taken off, which showed his left profile, since everything could be seen in the polished surface; on the other side was a mirror, which reflected the other profile of the naked man; which was a thing of most beautiful and bizarre fancy, whereby he sought to prove that painting does in fact, with more excellence, labour and effect, achieve more at one single view than does sculpture . . .".

According to Coletti [1955], this can be identified with the *St George* mentioned by Pino (see n.99) in spite of the differences that can be noticed in the two descriptions.

**111. Portrait of Caterina Cornaro.** Painted "from life" and belonging to Giovanni Cornaro in Venice. Also mentioned by Ridolfi [1648].

**112. Portrait of a Member of the House of Fugger.** The "head, coloured in oil" was in Vasari's book of drawings and showed "a German of the Fugger family, who was at that time one of the principal merchants in the Fondaco dei Tedeschi . . .". Mentioned also by Ridolfi, at Antwerp, in van Verle's house. See *Catalogue*, n.80.

## Carlo Ridolfi

*(Le Maraviglie . . .*, 1648.)

**113. Paintings on the outside of Grimani's**

*Drawings in the Ecole des Beaux-Arts, Paris: (top) Viola Player and (below) Head of an Old Man.*

**House.** On the façade of the house presumed to have been Giorgione's in Venice, in Campo S. Silvestro ". . . he painted within oval shapes some musicians, Poets and other fancies, and . . . groups of children . . . and in another part . . . two half-length figures said to represent the Emperor Frederick I and Antonia of Bergamo, the latter plunging a dagger into her side to kill herself in order to preserve her virginity . . . and lower down are two stories, whose subjects cannot be understood because time has so greatly damaged them". Boschini also quotes this passage [*Le Ricche Minere . . .*, 1674].

**114. Paintings on the outside of the Grimani House.** On the façade of the Venetian palace at Servi ". . . there still remain some nude women with beautiful figures and finely coloured". Boschini [1674] describes them as carried out by Titian and already in a ruined condition.

**115. Frescoes in Campo S. Stefano in Venice.** On the façade of a building: "half-length figures beautifully drawn". Boschini referred to them [1674] as having almost completely disappeared.

**116. Fresco Paintings at S. Maria Zobenigo in Venice.** On the façade of a house looking out over the canal: "in ovals, busts of Bacchus, Venus and Mars and grotesques in chiaroscuro at the sides and children". Boschini also describes them [1674].

**117. Three Figures.** In the possession of Paolo del Sera in Venice: "three portraits . . . on the same wood panel". Doubtfully identified with the *Concert* at the Pitti (n.33).

**118. Allegory of Human Life.** Quoted as belonging to the Cassinelli family in Genoa; consisting of half-length figures: nurse with child, armed warrior, "youth debating with philosophers, and among bargaining merchants and with a little old woman", and the nude figure of an old man.

**119. Self-portrait as David, with a Knight and a Soldier.** Mentioned as being in Andrea Vendramin's house in Venice; the knight and the soldier stand by David who carries Goliath's head. This picture cannot be identified with n.26 nor with n.76. Von Hadeln [in Ridolfi, 1914] draws attention to an illustration relating to this painting in the manuscript *De Picturis in Museis Andreae Vendramini*, in the British Museum, London (ms. Sloane, 4004, fol. 15).

**120. Bust of a Gipsy Woman.** It belonged to Giovanni Battista Sanudo (Venice): "half-length figure of a woman in gipsy costume", "her right hand resting on a printed book; Von Hadeln [in Ridolfi, 1914] identifies the painting with one of the Delphic Sibyl which Crowe and Cavalcaselle knew was owned by the Sorio family at franco".

Marostica [cf. F. Zanotto, *La Sibilla Delfica di . . . Giorgione*, 1856].

**121. David Offering Saul the Head of Goliath.** Mentioned as being in Leoni's house at S. Lorenzo in Venice.

**122. The Judgment of Solomon.** In the Grimani house at S. Marcuola, Venice. For the proposed identification, see n.70.

**123. Madonna with St Jerome and other Figures.** It belonged to the Senator Gussoni in Venice.

**124. Armed Knight.** The portrait of a "knight in black armour" is mentioned in the Contarini house in S. Samuele in Venice. It can perhaps be identified with one of the portraits of knights about which Vasari writes.

**125. Portrait of the Philosopher Luigi Crasso.** Mentioned as belonging to Niccolò Crasso in Venice (?) ". . . the portrait of Luigi Crasso, the celebrated Philosopher seated with his spectacles in his hand". Von Hadeln [in Ridolfi, 1914] pointed out, however, that the quotation is not very clear: no philosopher with the name of the sitter is known and Niccolò Crasso, who died in 1595, must have been a baby in Giorgione's day.

**126. St Sebastian.** Three-quarter length figure, owned by the Aldobrandini Princes in Rome.

**127. Young Man with a Suit of Armour.** In van Verle's house in Antwerp. One hand of the sitter is reflected in the armour.

**128. Male Nude.** Belonging to the van Verle family, ". . . the half-length figure of a naked man, deep in thought, with a green cloth on his knees and a breastplate on one side in which he is reflected . . ."

**129. Pope Alexander III Receives Homage from the Emperor Frederick.** In the large Council Chamber in the Doge's Palace: the Emperor Frederick is painted in the act of kissing the Pope's foot. The reference to the work on the other hand is expressed in vague terms: "Some people seem to think that [Giorgione] began this painting . . . (which others say was begun by Gio. Bellino), and was then finished by Titian . . .". The painting was one of the cycle devoted to the legendary war between Barbarossa and Alexander III. Various Venetian painters were engaged on the cycle and it was destroyed in the fire of 1577.

**130. Religious Subject.** The "portrait of a Christ in Majesty in antique style" is mentioned as being in Venice, but no other details about its whereabouts or the subject are given.

**131. Portrait of the Doge Agostino Barbarigo.** This painting is mentioned without stating its whereabouts, and this is the case for all the pictures listed below.

**132. The Castration of the Cats.** "On a large canvas a family is gathered together and

in their midst an old man, a huge hat shading half his face and a long beard with soft curls, is in the act of castrating a cat held on a woman's lap. She shows disgust and is turning her face away. A maid-servant . . . and a boy and a girl are present . . .".

**133. Nude Woman and Shepherd with a Flageolet.** "He painted also a naked woman and with her a shepherd playing a flageolet, and she was looking at him smiling . . .".

**134. Stories of Psyche.** A series of twelve paintings seen by Ridolfi, who describes each one in detail.

**135. The Ascent to Calvary.** ". . . a picture with half-length figures . . . of Christ led to Mount Calvary by many ruffianly soldiers . . . , the Marys and the virgin maid Veronica accompanied him and she stretched forward a linen cloth in order to gather the blood falling in precious drops".

**136. The Bust of Polyphemus Wearing a Large Hat.** ". . . a large Polyphemus with a huge hat on his head, which threw a bold shadow across his face . . .".

**137. Paintings for cassoni.** Ridolfi mentions nineteen illustrations of fables from Ovid, remarking that some of them "were reduced to small panels and various studies". The subjects given are: the golden age; the giants struck down by Jove's thunderbolt; Deucalion and Pyrrha; the serpent Python killed by Apollo; Apollo and Daphne; Io, Argus and Mercury; the fall of Phaeton; Diana and Callisto; Mercury and Apollo's flocks of sheep; Niobe and her sons slain by Apollo's darts; Baucis and Philemon; Theseus and Ariadne; Alcides, Dejanira and Nessus; Cupids and Apollo and Hyacinth; Cupids and Venus and Adonis. There is no mention of where they were to be seen except that the last mentioned painting was in Venice owned by the Vidmani family.

It is possible that these paintings can be identified with some small pictures, the subjects of which are not made clear (see n.54–58 in the *Catalogue*), and with many others of Giorgionesque character: particularly the illustration of *Apollo and Daphne*, see n.64. An engraving of the *Rape of Europa* is known from Teniers' *Theatrum Pictorium*.

## Other works presumed to be copies

**138. The Lovers.** Formerly belonged to the Borghese family in Rome; engraved in 1773 by Domenico Cunego for *Schola Italica* by Gavin Hamilton.

**139. Nude Woman and Cutthroat.** Known through a

painting by Teniers the Younger (canvas, 22 × 32; Gronau Collection, London), copied from a presumed prototype by Giorgione at Brussels, in the picture gallery of the Archduke Leopold William; the original was transferred later to Vienna and is mentioned until 1735; there is also an engraving in *Theatrum Pictorium*.

**140. Orpheus and Eurydice.** Bergamo, Accademia Carrara (Canvas 39 × 53). Attributed To Titian in the recent Museum Catalogue [Russoli, 1967]. Fiocco [1941] and Berenson [until 1957] thought, on the contrary, that it was an anonymous painting from a lost Giorgionesque original.

**141. Madonna in a Niche.** Leningrad, Hermitage. Copy by Francesco Vecellio (not entered in the Museum Catalogue [1958]).

**142. The Crossing of the Red Sea.** Venice, Accademia (Canvas 132 × 213). Painted by Andrea Previtali. Berenson [until 1957] considered it, and the following *Christ in Limbo*, as a copy of a lost original by Giorgione.

**143. Christ in Limbo.** Venice, Accademia (Canvas 132 × 213). Painting by Previtali. See n.142.

**144. Vulcan Tempers Cupid's Arrow.** Venice, Pinacoteca Querini Stampalia In Berenson's opinion [until 1957], this is a variant of about 1530 of a lost original.

## Other drawings attributed to Giorgione

**Callisto and Nymphs.** Paris, Louvre In red chalk (35 × 38). The drawing was cut out following the line of the figures. It is difficult to be certain that it is by Giorgione.

**Lucretia.** Zurich, Kunsthaus. In pencil and charcoal on brown paper (35 × 28.7).

**Female Nude, Back View.** Rotterdam, Boymans–van Beuningen Museum In thick pencil on brown paper (26.7 × 13.8).

**Landscape with River and Castle.** Rotterdam, Boymans–van Beuningen Museum. In pencil (27.2 × 15.8).

**Holy Family.** Vienna, Albertina Sepia painting (26 × 21.8). The attribution to Giorgione is apparently supported by W. Koschatzky and N. Keil [Catalogue 1966].

**Viola Player.** Paris, Ecole des Beaux-Arts Pen drawing (19.4 × 14.6). There is also a second figure near a tree trunk. Formerly attributed to Giulio Campagnola [Kristeller], and Tietze, Fiocco and Pignatti were of the same opinion. Hadeln suggests that Giorgione is the artist and this view is widely shared by Justi, Suida, Morassi and Coletti.

**Head of St Joseph.** Zurich, Schöni Collection Charcoal sketch on brown paper (21.5 × 13.5). There is a similar theme on the back carried out in the same medium.

**Head of an Old Man.** Paris, Ecole des Beaux-Arts It was at first thought to be by Perugino; A. Venturi attributed

it to Giorgione, comparing it with the *Three Philosophers* in Vienna (n.17). Coletti agreed but Morassi appears doubtful. Pignatti detects in it characteristics of Lotto. Together with another folio sheet in the same collection (see above), it is amongst those drawings most plausibly related to the master.

# Indexes
## Index of titles and subjects

*103*

## Topographical Index